PROVOCATIONS

THE MYTH OF MERITOCRACY

WHY WORKING-CLASS KIDS GET WORKING-CLASS JOBS

JAMES BLOODWORTH

SERIES EDITOR:
YASMIN ALIBHAI-BROWN

Biteback Publishing

First published in Great Britain in 2016 by
Biteback Publishing Ltd
Westminster Tower
3 Albert Embankment
London SE1 7SP
Copyright © James Bloodworth 2016

ISBN 978-1-78590-053-2

10 9 8 7 6 5 4 3 2 1

A CIP catalogue record for this book is available from the British Library.

Set in Stempel Garamond by Adrian McLaughlin

Printed and bound in Great Britain by
CPI Group (UK) Ltd, Croydon CR0 4YY

MIX
Paper from
responsible sources
FSC
www.fsc.org   FSC® C020471

MERITOCRACY

/ˌmer.əˈtɑː.krə.si/

*'a social system, society, or organisation in which
people have power because of their abilities, not
because of their money or social position'*

*'This haphazard Mobocracy ... must be replaced by
a democratic aristocracy: that is by the dictatorship,
not of the whole proletariat, but of that 5 per cent
of it capable of conceiving the job and pioneering
in the drive towards its divine goal'.*[1]

—GEORGE BERNARD SHAW

---

1   *The Rise of the Meritocracy*, Michael Young, Pelican Books (1958).

Part

Part I

TURNING BRITAIN INTO a meritocracy is a modern political obsession. Seldom do today's politicians talk about reducing economic inequality; instead they prefer to ruminate on 'aspiration', viewing it as their job to ensure that the most talented people rise to the top – and reap the financial rewards in the process. When the late Michael Young, author of Labour's portentous 1945 election manifesto and inspiration behind the Open University, coined the word meritocracy back in 1958, it was intended as a warning. Young's fictional essay *The Rise of the Meritocracy* had imagined a Britain of the future in which a meritocratic elite had replaced the old aristocratic order. British society had hitherto 'condemned even talented people to manual work'. Young's imagined utopia had upended all of that and anointed a new elite that was no longer an 'aristocracy of birth' or a 'plutocracy of wealth', but a 'true meritocracy of talent' whose superior IQs were revealed through a process of rigorous examination.

Yet, rather than ushering in a harmonious new order of brotherhood and fraternity, equality of opportunity in Young's utopia meant equality of opportunity to be unequal. The supposed cranial superiority of the new elite was used by the new order to justify the gulf between it and wider society. In a grimly familiar twist, utopia bore a strong resemblance to dystopia, and the impetus to look after those wretched folk who languished at the bottom of society had evaporated like steam from a kettle. As for the supposed self-made men who sat atop this new meritocratic pile, all rich men in the new society had earned their fortune and were thus permitted to enjoy the extravagant rewards as they saw fit. No need to worry about charity for the destitute. The poor were ragged and wretched because their lowly IQs had made them that way. They had forfeited the right to look on resentfully at those above them the moment they had failed the 11-plus.

The old aristocratic order – which the new society had finally swept away – had evoked the spurious concept of good breeding to justify its position and influence. With its passing, a new and meritorious elite had come to power; and this one rationalised its dominance on the basis of rigorous and scientific IQ testing.

The Rise of the Meritocracy was, as Young would later write, 'a satire meant to be a warning (which needless to say has not been heeded) against what might happen to Britain between the year 1958 and the imagined final revolt against meritocracy in 2003'.[2] Young claimed that he 'wanted to show how overweening a meritocracy could be'. What is surprising today is just how many politicians appear to have taken Young's work not as a cautionary tale but as an ideological blueprint. *IQ + Effort = Merit* – that was the state ideology in Young's dystopian England, where equality of opportunity had finally become a reality. Today it is a formulation that politicians of all stripes have adopted as the ideal – even those who, as the soldier turned socialist Richard Tawney

---

2   'Down with Meritocracy', Michael Young, *The Guardian*, 29 June 2001.

put it in the '30s, 'resist most strenuously attempts to apply it'.[3] Young himself recognised the irony of this in the years after *The Rise of the Meritocracy* was first published. 'It hasn't been taken as a warning but a sort of blessing,' he told an interviewer in 1994.[4]

In few places has the goal of meritocracy been adopted with quite the same vigour as in the upper echelons of the modern Conservative Party. Prime Minister David Cameron says he wants to see

> a more socially mobile Britain ... where no matter where you come from ... you can get to the top in tele-vision, you can get to the top in the judiciary, get to the top of the armed services, get to the top in politics and get to the top in newspapers.

Cameron made the same point more succinctly in 2013 when he stated that 'I believe in equality of

---

3   *Equality*, R. H. Tawney, Unwin Books, 3rd edition (1975).

4   *The Rise and Rise of Meritocracy*, edited by Geoff Dench, Wiley-Blackwell, 1st edition (2006).

opportunity'.[5] Both Cameron and his Chancellor of the Exchequer George Osborne have talked repeatedly about helping 'strivers' and those who 'aspire to get on'. These upwardly mobile flag-bearers of the meritocracy have typically been contrasted with 'shirkers' – the Burberry-clad layabouts who supposedly skulk behind net curtains glancing fearfully at their aspirational peers as the latter head off to work. With the creation of a meritocracy in mind, in 2008 the Conservatives released a report entitled 'Through the Glass Ceiling: A Conservative Agenda for Social Mobility'. The Liberal Democrats share this aspiration. The former party leader Nick Clegg claimed in 2012 that social mobility was the coalition government's 'central social preoccupation'.[6] The culmination of this rhetoric was a cross-departmental strategy published in 2011 with the central claim that 'improving social mobility is the principal goal of the government's social policy'.

---

5   'David Cameron brushes Boris Johnson aside over IQ comments', Tomas Jivanda, *The Independent*, 2 December 2013.

6   Nick Clegg, speech to the Sutton Trust, 22 May 2012.

The Labour Party has also seemingly accepted the desirability of a meritocracy, with former leader Ed Miliband telling the Sutton Trust conference in 2012 that social mobility 'must not be just about changing the odds that young people from poor backgrounds will make it to university ... we also have to improve opportunities for everyone, including those who don't go to university'.[7] Shadow Cabinet member Jon Trickett had a similar message when he said in the same year that Labour 'should be the engine of social mobility'.[8]

Like universal suffrage and world peace, every politician in modern Britain purports to be in favour of meritocracy.

For most of Britain's history, young people have grown up with a keen sense of their station in life. Historically, Britain has been a country with a rigid class system, where education was a luxury afforded only to a small minority. Until the late nineteenth century, children

---

7   'Ed Miliband attacks social inequality', Martha Linden and James Tapsfield, *The Independent*, 21 May 2012.

8   'Wanted by Labour, working-class MPs', Michael Savage, *The Times*, 16 July 2012.

of the rich and powerful attended exclusive public and grammar schools, while churches and charity schools provided a rudimentary education for the lower classes. In practice this meant that the lives of talented working-class people were often wasted in ignorance and drudgery.

Things only really began to change (and even then very slowly) with the passage of the 1870 Education Act, the first piece of legislation committed to providing education on a national scale. The policy was driven by Liberal MP William Forster and enacted at a time when the political establishment in Britain was beginning to grasp the frivolity of consigning intelligent children to penury and toil. However, the new law was not intro-duced as an act of generosity; rather, it was thought that by fully exploiting the talents of the many rather than the few Britain would better be able to compete with its emerging economic rivals.

The initial passage of the act was far from smooth. While mainstream Conservatives would eventually come to recognise the benefits of education in terms of keeping Britain economically competitive, many initially worried that educating the poor would lead them off the straight and narrow. The poor might, after all, use their newly stimulated cerebral matter to imbibe subversive literature and, as a consequence, get ideas above their station. And so, during a debate in the House of Commons in 1807, the Tory MP Davies Gilbert warned the House that 'giving education to the working classes would be bad for their morals and happiness. It would lead them to despise their lot in life instead of making them good servants in agriculture and other work to which their rank in society had destined them…'[9]

Even among those seeking reform, educating the poor was typically framed in terms of how it would benefit capitalists, rather than how it might improve the lot of workers. Introducing his own policy, William Forster warned that if the British workforce remained unskilled, 'they will become overmatched in the competition of the world'.[10] In the eighteenth century, Adam Smith, champion of the free market and author of the influential *The Wealth of Nations*, argued along similar lines in

9   Hansard, HC Deb, 13 July 1807, vol. 30, cc. 1007–48.

10   Hansard, HC Deb, 17 July 1873, vol. 217, cc. 502–90.

favour of educating the poor. For proponents of the free market, nepotism and Britain's rigid social order were impediments to an efficient economy. The best jobs invariably went not to those in possession of the most brilliant minds but to the well-connected or to the progeny of the wealthiest families. The problem for free marketeers wasn't so much inequity as inefficiency. However talented they might be, nepotism discouraged those placed lower in society from ever attempting anything that smacked of aspiration.

Conservative politicians and thinkers would eventually reconcile themselves to the views of MPs like William Forster, at least in terms of educating the poor. No Tory MP would dare to stand up in the House of Commons today and claim that the poor should be denied education lest it make them 'difficult'. Recent Conservative governments have appeared (on the surface, at least) to take social mobility just as seriously as their political rivals in the Labour Party. Ramsay Muir, a journalist and leading member of the post-war Liberal Party, summed up this interpretation of the meritocratic ideal well when he said that the state should not 'establish an artificial equality among men who are naturally unequal and different. The only forms of equality which it will pursue will be equality before the law, and equality of opportunities for all citizens to make the most of their varying powers.'[11]

Contrary to theories purporting to show an unbreakable affiliation between the Conservative Party and the aristocratic 'establishment', the *raison d'être* of the Thatcher governments was actually to do away with the old and anoint a new aristocracy based on a grasping *get-rich-quick* notion of getting on. Instead of knowing one's place, as old Tories like Mr Gilbert would undoubtedly have preferred, during Mrs Thatcher's time as Prime Minister the most avaricious were encouraged to rise even if they had begun life among the working classes. Under Thatcher, you were not despised if you scrambled up from the very bottom; rather, you were assumed to be useless if you did not. Money, rather than the specious concept of breeding, was king in the 1980s.

---

11 *Liberalism Divided: A Study in British Political Thought 1914–1939*, Michael Freeden, Oxford University Press, 1st edition (1986).

Of course, Britain is a long way from being a society with the levels of social mobility seen in *The Rise of the Meritocracy*. Fears of impending meritocratic dystopia are therefore unwarranted. Yet there is something disconcerting about the way a concept conceived of as having potentially dystopian consequences has been adopted by politicians as a sacred goal. The Conservatives, in their economically liberal incarnation, have long purported to favour the creation of a meritocracy, as have their friends in the corporate world. Investment banking giant Goldman Sachs even informs potential recruits on its website that 'Goldman Sachs is a meritocracy'. What has changed is that today the Labour Party too is supportive of the meritocratic ideal – or, as Labour politicians prefer to call it, 'equality of opportunity'.

This brings to mind an anecdote told by the recently deceased journalist and author Christopher Hitchens. On visiting totalitarian North Korea, Hitchens once joked that, such was the scale of the repression and leader worship in that country, it was as if the Kims had been handed a dog-eared copy of George Orwell's *Nineteen Eighty-Four* and been told to make it work.

Something similar might be said of British politicians and Young's satirical essay on meritocracy. Rather than taking Young's tome as a warning against a bleak and grossly unequal future, politicians of both right and left have embraced it. Twenty-first-century social democracy will defend to the death your right to be unequal to the next man – as long as merit, rather than wealth, has placed you on your allotted rung of the ladder. Young's oracular warning of half a century ago has been recast as a blueprint.

Part II

WHEN ASKED IN 2002 what her greatest achievement in government was, the former Conservative Prime Minister Margaret Thatcher is said to have replied, 'Tony Blair and New Labour. We forced our opponents to change their minds.'[12] Thatcher's electoral dominance in the 1980s obliged Labour to transform the offering *it* was putting to the electorate every four or five years. By the time Labour was finally elected in 1997, after eighteen years in opposition, the party had dropped commitments to unilateral nuclear disarmament and to the nationalisation

---

12 'Margaret Thatcher's greatest achievement: New Labour', Conor Burns, Conservative Home, 11 April 2008.

of industry. Perhaps more significantly, New Labour under Blair was also committed to maintaining the previous Conservative government's spending plans during its first term in office and to freezing the top rate of income tax. Related to this was Labour's conversion to the principle of 'equality of opportunity' over equality of outcome. Labour had finally accepted the desirability of meritocracy.

Sections of the Labour Party had of course leant towards the narrower goal of social mobility prior to the birth of New Labour. As the Labour MP Anthony Crosland wrote in his influential 1956 book *The Future of Socialism*: 'Some radicals ... would be content with the strictly limited objective of equal opportunity [over greater economic equality].' Yet, until the advent of New Labour, the mainstream of the party was intent on raising the working class as a whole, rather than simply plucking the most meritorious from its ranks. Opportunity was seen as a collective right rather than an individual one, and was wedded to the socialist ideal of a classless society.

By the time Labour came to power in 1997, those

whom Crosland had once described dismissively as 'some radicals' were in the ascendant. The doctrine of equality of opportunity had, as Crosland noted, always had its proponents in Labour circles. Yet it was the birth of New Labour that finally cemented the goal of a meritocratic society as, on the surface at least, a cross-party aspiration. Labour politics had traditionally placed a strong emphasis on, if not the utopian goal of complete economic equality, then at least on a narrowing of the gap between rich and poor. Thus Crosland, viewed in his time as coming from the right of the Labour Party, wrote in 1956 that 'by equality we meant more than a meritocratic society of equal opportunities, in which the greatest rewards would go to those with the most fortunate genetic endowment and family background ... We also meant more than a simple (not that it has proved simple in practice) redistribution of income.'[13] The New Labour project quietly discarded this egalitarian ethos and replaced it (although they would surely argue that

---

13   *The Future of Socialism*, Anthony Crosland, Jonathan Cape, 3rd edition
      (1956).

they were updating it) with the idea of equality of opportunity. The new goal was summed up neatly in 1998 by Peter Mandelson, when he famously claimed that New Labour was 'intensely relaxed about people getting filthy rich, as long as they pay their taxes'. Put another way, it was no longer important how much money tycoons and the high-fliers took home, as long as tax revenues were used to make life easier for those living in poverty. For New Labour, taxing the rich heavily would have been punitive and counterproductive. Instead, it chose to use the proceeds of a booming City of London to build a more generous social safety net. A loosely regulated City would drive growth, which would in turn push up tax revenues that could be spent on the poor. Tony Blair's ideal was not socialism but rather social mobility – or 'social-ism', as Blair liked to call it.

This represented the politics of the so-called third way, a blend of right-wing economics and left-wing social policies. According to the sociologist Anthony Giddens, one of the architects of third-way thinking, this apparent compromise between workers and capital favoured economic growth and dynamism but was also committed to social justice.[14] Making social democracy more business-friendly was a central tenet of third-way thought. As such, it came ready-made for a generation of rising New Labour stars who wanted to break with the left's statist past. Beyond New Labour, social democrats abroad were also attracted by the politics of the third way after suffering numerous political defeats at the hands of a resurgent conservatism in the 1980s. Similar assumptions to those which animated New Labour – of a historic compromise between workers and capital – were wedded to the doctrines of socialist and social democratic parties across the West in the early 1990s, most notably in the United States under Democratic President Bill Clinton.

As a consequence of its adherence to the third way, in government New Labour shied away from policies associated with reducing the gap between rich and poor, such as higher taxes on top earners. Instead, Labour focused

---

14 Though, in 2007, Giddens appeared to row back on some of the assumptions of the Blair era, writing in *The Guardian* that 'reducing inequality and creating greater chances of mobility are not alternatives, but are interdependent'.

on ameliorating the dark underbelly of the free market, epitomised by widespread child and pensioner poverty. Blair in fact slapped down Commons Leader Peter Hain in 2003 after the Labour Member of Parliament for Neath suggested that the richest in society should contribute more in tax. Blair's response to Hain's betrayal of New Labour orthodoxy perfectly captured the meritocratic ideal. 'My concern is not to penalise the people who are successful and doing well and earning a lot of money,' Blair said. 'My concern is to lift up the incomes of those who are at the lower end of the income scale.'[15]

It is, at this point, worth recalling a 2001 report by the government's Performance and Innovation Unit (also known as the Prime Minister's Strategy Unit). The report focused on improving upward social mobility for children from poor backgrounds. Importantly, it also looked at how to reduce barriers to downward social mobility for dull middle-class children. Predictably, some of the policy options that came out of the report, such as an increase in inheritance tax, were seen

---

15 'Hain's tax call angers Blair', This Is Money, 20 June 2003.

as unpalatable to New Labour. As a result, the report was quietly dropped.

Nor, during its time in office, did New Labour make any attempt to knock Britain's private schools off their perch. Indeed, New Labour politicians often had a vested interest in maintaining educational inequalities. For his eldest son Euan, Tony Blair opted for the prestigious London Oratory, a high-performing faith school in Fulham with nearly twice the average number of good GCSE passes and only 6 per cent of pupils from deprived homes.[16] Particularly revealing was a conversation Blair had with the late Robin Cook MP that was documented in Cook's memoirs. Cook and former Labour Deputy Leader Roy Hattersley were in conversation with Blair one day about the latter's choice of a selective school for his eldest son. In a principled defence of comprehensive education, the two Labour grandees informed the Prime Minister that Harold Wilson had sent his children to a comprehensive and one had gone on to

16 'State school where Blair sent two of his sons ordered to stop excluding the poor after being accused of discrimination', Wills Robinson, *Daily Mail*, 16 July 2014.

become a headmaster and the other a university professor. 'I rather hope my sons do better than that!' replied
Blair, betraying both the ultra-high aspirations he had
for his own children and his apparent disdain for comprehensive schooling.

Spending on public services gradually increased in
Labour's second and third terms (during Blair's first term
in government, public spending as a percentage of GDP
actually fell),[17] but New Labour's time in government
was characterised by a hands-off approach to the super-
rich. As a consequence, economic inequalities unleashed
by eighteen years of Conservative rule were aggravated.
Government statistics show that between 1997 and 2010,
the real-terms gap in income between the highest and
lowest earners grew by £237 per week.[18] According to
figures from the Department for Work and Pensions,
the incomes of the poorest 10 per cent of UK households grew by just £24 per week in real terms over New

---

17 'Public spending', bbc.co.uk, 11 May 2001, http://news.bbc.co.uk/news/
vote2001/hi/english/main_issues/sections/facts/newsid_1146000/1146798.stm.

18 'Inequality: where New Labour really did "crash the car"', James Bloodworth,
Left Foot Forward, 8 October 2014.

Labour's thirteen years in power, compared with an increase of £256 per week for the richest 10 per cent.[19]

Yet, while inequality may not have been reined in by New Labour, there was a committed attack on poverty. The excesses of the rich during the Blair and Brown years have made it fashionable to retrospectively dismiss the New Labour project as a pale imitation of the Conservative Party. With respect to the poor, such arguments do not stand up to even a modicum of scrutiny. Under Blair and Brown there was a serious drive to improve the lot of Britain's most economically vulnerable citizens. New Labour spent significant sums of money on public services and on policies such as tax credits for low-paid workers. Light-touch regulation of the banks was accompanied by Sure Start Centres for underprivileged children and record spending on the National Health Service. As a result of these spending priorities, both absolute and relative income poverty fell significantly among both children and pensioners between 1997 and 2010.

---

19 'Living Standards, Inequality and Poverty: Labour's Record', Alastair Muriel, David Phillips and Luke Sibieta, Institute for Fiscal Studies, 2010 Election Briefing Note No. 2.

This was not simply the fruit of a booming economy, but the result of deliberate spending decisions taken by successive New Labour governments. Tony Blair promised to end child poverty within a generation and Gordon Brown pledged 'to end pensioner poverty in our country'. These goals were reflected in the choices New Labour made on spending. Between 1997/98 and 2010/11, there was an £18 billion annual increase in spending on benefits for families with children and an £11 billion annual increase on benefits for pensioners.[20]

With respect to ameliorating poverty, New Labour was only the same as the Thatcher and Major governments in the sense that a goldfish is the same as a shark.

Yet, as we have seen, New Labour represented a discernible shift in emphasis in terms of how the left treated inequality. Instead of striving for a greater equalisation of economic outcomes, as in Labour's past, the theoretical underpinning of New Labour stressed equality of opportunity over equality of outcome. This ideological

---

20 'Labour's record on poverty and inequality', Robert Joyce and Luke Sibieta, Institute for Fiscal Studies, 6 June 2013.

metamorphosis was born of both electoral expediency and the need to update Labour's guiding philosophy for the twenty-first century. For New Labour's architects, a rebranding of the party was seen as critical if Labour was to climb back into government after nearly two decades in the electoral wilderness. As the late political consultant Philip Gould wrote in his influential New Labour text *The Unfinished Revolution*, a central aim of Labour's modernisers was to make the party less hostile to the sorts of people who 'want to do better for themselves and their families'.[21]

Broader historical trends also played a part in Labour's ideological transmutation. When the Berlin Wall came down in 1989, a blow was struck not only against the totalitarian delusions of communists, but also against the faint hopes of some on the left that economic planning could be made to work if only the right people were put in charge. Remove the ugly trappings of communist dictatorship but maintain the dominant role of the state in economic life and, so some maintained, socialism

---

21 *The Unfinished Revolution*, Philip Gould, Little, Brown, 1st edition (1998).

would flourish as surely as night follows day. The fall of communism – and more importantly the failure of economic planning – delivered a *coup de grâce* to that idea.

For those on the social democratic left who never had been enamoured of planning, the putrefaction of the social democratic consensus in the 1970s led to a similar ideological impasse. The middle period of the twentieth century had seen the state in the ascendant. In contrast, as the 1960s became the 1970s, it was impossible not to notice the flaws in the centre-left status quo. Nationalised industries had become inefficient behemoths that were heavily reliant on government subsidies. The left may lament the legacy of Margaret Thatcher, yet even the Labour governments of the 1970s recognised that the post-war settlement was coming unstuck.

The dogma of equality of opportunity provided New Labour with the ideological creed with which to assail opponents on both the left and the right. To the left, New Labour emphasised that the world had changed, and highlighted the ease with which a globalised financial elite could pack their bags and leave Britain when assailed by higher taxes. This, along with grim electoral reality, made the pursuit of economic equality a political dead end – or so argued New Labour's architects. What mattered instead was improving the lot of those at the bottom of society. To the right, New Labour claimed to be able to run the meritocracy more effectively than the increasingly incompetent Conservatives. Despite a decade of Thatcherism, the Tories were still seen by many as the party of the old aristocratic elite. One happy consequence of this metamorphosis was that Labour would no longer frighten the aspirational middle classes at the ballot box. Both Labour and the Conservatives were promising social mobility; yet it was New Labour who seemed to really mean it.

Thereafter, the 'm' word peppered Blair's speeches. 'We are light years from being a true meritocracy,' Blair lamented in 1995, only to declare a mere two years later, when in government, that 'the Britain of the elite is over. The new Britain is a meritocracy.' Blair was to return to this theme repeatedly during his time as Prime Minister. 'The old establishment is being replaced by a new, larger, more meritocratic middle class,' he claimed in January 1999. 'The meritocracy is built on the potential of the many, not the few' (October 1999); 'The meritocratic society is the only one that can exploit its economic potential to the full for all its people' (June 2000). As *The Guardian* reported in 2004, the spread of social mobility between the classes would be 'the cornerstone of his third term'. Blair defined his vision of Britain as 'an opportunity society'.[22]

As a consequence of Labour's new aspirational ethos, during his premiership Blair did not allow the top income tax rate to rise above 40 per cent. Meanwhile, the Labour Chancellor Gordon Brown cut capital gains tax to just 18 per cent. It was no longer important how much money those at the top made. What mattered instead was giving those at the bottom a leg up so that they too could enjoy the glittering prizes on offer in Labour's socially mobile meritocracy. Under New Labour, those who prospered would do so based on merit; however, once they had scaled the dizzy heights they would be cheered on by Labour grandees as they guiltlessly enjoyed the increasingly dazzling rewards.

---

22 'Blair to bank on social mobility', Patrick Wintour, *The Guardian*, 12 October 2004.

Part III

AS WELL AS extolling the desirability of a meritocracy, politicians like to contrast the supposed decline of social mobility in the present with an apparently golden age of opportunity during the twentieth century. In this hoary old tale, the post-war period is romantically cast as an era when the lowly were permitted to rise – if not seamlessly then at least doggedly – through the ranks of British society and up into the top jobs. Anecdotal evidence is often marshalled to drive the point home. Politics today is supposedly dominated by the progeny of the country's most prestigious fee-paying schools. The former Labour Prime Minister Harold Wilson went to a grammar school, whereas sitting Prime Minister David Cameron is a descendant of King William IV and attended Eton. Popular culture is increasingly the preserve of young men and women with posh accents and trust funds – things also seemingly possessed by almost everyone working in the media.

From this apparently unimpeachable set of assumptions, several things are commonly deduced: social mobility has stalled or is in reverse; there was a higher level of social mobility after the Second World War; and the way to reverse this trend is to improve things like education for poorer pupils.

It is mostly the left that makes the broader argument about social mobility going into reverse, though some on the right have hit upon the same point too. So Frances O'Grady, the General Secretary of the TUC, has described Britain as a '*Downton Abbey*-style society' in which social mobility 'has hit reverse'.[23] The former New Labour minister Alan Milburn, chair of the government's Child Poverty and Social Mobility

---

23 'Britain "becoming like Downton Abbey" says TUC leader', Justin Parkinson, bbc.co.uk, 8 September 2014.

Commission, similarly argued in 2009 that certain professions were a 'closed shop' where 'birth, not worth, has become more and more a determinant of people's life chances'. Like other commentators, Milburn contrasted an apparently worsening level of social mobility today with a period during the last century when 'the professions created unheard-of opportunities for millions of men and women'.[24] On the right, the former Conservative Prime Minister Sir John Major has similarly claimed that 'in every single sphere of British influence, the upper echelons of power ... are held overwhelmingly by the privately educated or the affluent middle class'.[25] Sir John described this as a 'collapse in social mobility' which, rather predictably, he blamed on Labour.

It is worth asking, then: was there really a postwar golden era of social mobility when the children of

---

24 'Unleashing Aspiration: The Final Report of the Panel on Fair Access to the Professions', 21 July 2009.

25 '"Truly shocking" that the private-school educated and affluent middle class still run Britain, says Sir John Major', Christopher Hope, *Daily Telegraph*, 10 November 2013.

factory workers could effortlessly rise to the very top? And if so, what has gone wrong since then?

There are a few things to bear in mind when reflecting on this commonly heard lament. Firstly, there are two categories of social mobility, and understanding the difference between the two goes some way to explaining why social mobility appears to have been so much better in the second half of the twentieth century. On the one hand, there is *individual* mobility. This is where one person moves up the ladder and another moves down. Apart from at times of rapid social change, there are a finite number of places in each social class – thus one person must move down in order to free up a place higher up for someone else to move up. In contrast, periods of economic change create something called *structural* mobility. As an industrial society becomes a consumer society, so the number of white-collar jobs invariably increases. The expansion of the professions – and the inevitable movement into these jobs of a generation whose parents may have worked in industry – creates a high degree of structural mobility. The structure of the economy changes and as a consequence there is more room at the top.

In the second half of the twentieth century, there was a large expansion in the number of middle-class and white-collar jobs, and so it stands to reason that there should be a corresponding fall in the number of people categorised as traditional working class. Hence the widespread impression of, as Milburn put it, 'opportunities for millions of men and women'.

According to one influential piece of research, the perceived collapse in social mobility in recent times appears to have been illusory. The Nuffield Mobility Study, carried out from 1968 to 1971, found that while there was a significant degree of upward mobility in Britain during the post-war period, this was mainly due to the expansion of middle-class and professional occupations. In other words, there was an increase in the type of structural mobility already mentioned. The apparent golden era of social mobility in the mid-twentieth century was to some extent deceptive. The expansion of white-collar professions created more room at the top – and thus more structural social mobility. The rate at which the children of working-class parents are being pulled into the middle classes by a changing economy is slower today; and social mobility therefore appears to have slowed with it. A further 2010 paper by Goldthorpe and Erikson found that, rather than social mobility going into reverse for those born after 1970, it was actually the high level of economic mobility prior to that which was unusual.

However, measuring social mobility in a different way leads to a rather different conclusion.

By looking at mobility between income groups – as opposed to measuring it between social classes, as the Nuffield researchers did – it is possible to compare the incomes of those born in the 1970s with the incomes of their parents. One piece of research conducted by economists at the Centre for Economic Performance at the London School of Economics did just that – and reached very different conclusions to the Nuffield study. Looking at the relationship between family income and children's later earnings, the researchers at LSE found that intergenerational mobility 'fell markedly over time in Britain', with those born in 1970 'substantially' less individually mobile than those born in 1958. According to this study, in recent times the links between child and parent economic status 'appear to have strengthened considerably'.[26] There have also been sharp drops in cross-generation mobility of economic status between the cohorts. In other words, social mobility has regressed just like the doom-mongers claim. The authors of the report attributed this fall to 'the increasing relationship between family income and educational attainment'. They also noted that the decline in social mobility had occurred at a time of increasing income inequality. They added that there was greater intergenerational mobility between income groups in more egalitarian societies like Canada and the Nordic countries. In countries with high levels of inequality, such as Britain and the United States, intergenerational mobility was 'at the lower end of international comparisons'.

So who to believe?

It isn't easy to measure social mobility because doing so requires studies that track people over long periods of time. Different methods of measuring social mobility

---

26 'Intergenerational Mobility in Europe and North America', Jo Blanden, Paul Gregg and Stephen Machin, Centre for Economic Performance, LSE, April 2005.

tend to produce different results. Thus caution should be exercised with respect to confident proclamations that social mobility in Britain is in precipitous decline.[27]

There is evidence today to suggest that there is a good deal of social mobility in the middle of society, and considerably less at the extremes. Britain remains a country in which it is exceedingly difficult to go from stacking shelves in a supermarket to the boardroom of a top company. It is at the extremes where measuring mobility between economics groups (as seen in the LSE study) is a more effective method of understanding what is going on than measuring mobility between the social classes. Income differentiation within classes is increasingly important when a small section of the elite appears to be pulling away from the rest. Using the aforementioned economic categories, Professor Mike Savage of the LSE analysed the Great British Class Survey (GBCS) – a 2011 survey of 160,000 British residents – and found that the elite today is far more exclusive than any of the

---

27 'Has social mobility in Britain decreased? Reconciling divergent findings on income and class mobility', Robert Erikson and John H. Goldthorpe, *The British Journal of Sociology*, 2010, vol. 61, issue 2.

other social classes.[28] Or at least most of it is. Among the more traditional occupations – barristers, CEOs, judges and financial intermediaries – income differences by origin are especially pronounced. By contrast, the technical professions – scientists, accountants, engineers, IT workers and academics – appear to be more open to those who have started life nearer the bottom of the ladder. Meanwhile, the more traditional occupations have also been found to pay more extravagant salaries. Within the same professions, higher rewards are conferred on those from the most privileged backgrounds for doing the same jobs. As Professor Savage puts it, 'Average incomes are highest among those jobs in which their personnel are most likely to be recruited from the most privileged families.'[29]

Inequality in Britain has unarguably increased over the past thirty-five years. Those who believe that social mobility has also decreased are inclined to view the

28 'About the Great British Class Survey', http://www.bbc.co.uk/labuk/articles/class.

29 *Social Class in the 21st Century*, Professor Mike Savage, Pelican Books, 1st edition (2015).

relationship as causal – growing inequality has hampered social mobility. Yet the link between growing inequality in Britain and falling social mobility is sketchy. As already mentioned, much depends on which study one looks at.

That said, a large body of research from the US appears to have uncovered evidence that falling social mobility can be linked to growing inequality. Importantly, this research covers a long enough period to exclude purely structural explanations. Undertaken by the economists Daniel Aaronson and Bhashkar Mazumder and looking at the period between 1940 and 2000, the study found that, when the rich got richer relative to the poor, social mobility fell.[30] The authors of the Intergenerational Economic Mobility in the US study concluded that 'mobility increased from 1950 to 1980 but has declined sharply since 1980'. They added that the recent decline in social mobility was 'only partially explained

---

30 'Intergenerational Economic Mobility in the U.S., 1940 to 2000', Daniel Aaronson and Bhashkar Mazumder, Federal Reserve Bank of Chicago, February 2007, http://www.chicagofed.org/digital_assets/publications/working_papers/2005/wp2005_12.pdf.

by education'. On analysing household income data, economists at the Boston Federal Reserve also found that social mobility in the US had declined since the 1970s.[31] Whereas 36 per cent of families remained in the same income decile throughout that decade, by the 1980s the figure had risen to 37 per cent and by the 1990s it had jumped again to 40 per cent. During this period, inequality also grew. Between 1979 and 2007, America's Gini index measure increased from 0.32 to 0.37.[32] The total share of US income going to the top 0.1 per cent increased from 0.8 per cent in 1973 to 6 per cent in 2007.[33] Meanwhile, the average income of the top 0.01 per cent increased almost nine-fold, from $4 million to $35 million.[34]

---

31   'Trends in U.S. Family Income Mobility, 1967–2004', Katherine Bradbury and Jane Katz, Federal Reserve Bank of Boston, 2009, http://bostonfed.org/economic/wp/wp2009/wp0907.htm.

32   'The United States: High and Rapidly Rising Inequality', Lane Kenworthy and Timothy Smeeding, July 2014, https://lanekenworthy.files.wordpress.com/2014/07/2014highandrapidlyrisinginequality.pdf.

33   'Income Inequality', Marc Priester and Aaron Mendelson, Inequality.org, http://inequality.org/income-inequality/#sthash.fxNqn4JD.dpuf.

34   'Why Elites Fail', Christopher Hayes, *The Nation*, 6 June 2012.

An expansion in the number of low-paid jobs in recent times (as well as a subsequent decline in the number of professional and managerial positions) appears to have increased the risk of downward mobility in Britain, too. In 2016, there is simply more room at the bottom. This was revealed in a comprehensive 2014 study published in the *British Journal of Sociology*. The study looked at more than 20,000 British men and women over four birth cohorts: from 1946, 1958, 1970 and 1980–84. It found that structural social mobility, which at one time propelled many working-class kids up into the professions, appeared today to be working in the opposite direction. Rather than stalling, social mobility is as much a reality as it was in the past – however, today it is transporting more people down the ladder rather than up. The study[35] also found that inequalities in the relative chances of mobility were greater than previously thought, with a child of professional parents twenty times more likely to get a high-status job than a working-class child.

---

35 'Decline in professional jobs fuels increase in downward mobility', Patrick Butler, *The Guardian*, 6 November 2014.

As we have seen, what looks in retrospect like a highly socially mobile society in the post-war period was in reality an economy in transition. More children from working-class families were swept up into the professions because the professions were hungrily swallowing up more and more people. As this trend slowed, social mobility slowed with it. This settling down of the economic climate is responsible for at least some of our perceptions about the betrayal of a golden age of social mobility.

Yet there is evidence that, as inequality has soared in recent decades, the elite has become more exclusive and un-meritocratic. This perhaps goes some way to explaining the widespread assumption that social mobility is in reverse: we see a good deal of the elite on our television screens and are thus liable to assume that the 'stickiness' of their social position reflects a collapse in mobility right across society. Similarly, at the other end of the ladder, the so-called precariat has become even more entrenched. The stereotypical images of Burberry-clad twenty-somethings trapped on benefits have come to denote a country in a parlous state of social stagnation.

Relative to other comparable nations, social mobility in Britain is poor. According to the OECD,[36] Britain has some of the lowest rates of social mobility in the developed world. In the UK, a person's earnings are more likely to reflect their father's than in any other country.

Whether this is a feature of the last thirty years or the last 300, it is no less shameful.

---

36 'A Family Affair: Intergenerational Social Mobility across OECD Countries', oecd.org, 2010, http://www.oecd.org/tax/public-finance/chapter%205%20 gfg%202010.pdf.

Part IV

SUPERMODEL KATE MOSS and her half-sister Lottie made history in August 2014 when they became the first siblings to grace the cover of fashion magazine *Vogue*. Big sister Kate, who has appeared on the front page of *Vogue* thirty-five times during her glittering modelling career, had been taking a 'keen interest in her sixteen-year-old half-sister's budding career', as one *Daily Mail* journalist noted at the time.[37] And Lottie's entrance into the world of modelling was already filled with promise. Several months prior to the siblings' ground-breaking *Vogue* shoot, Lottie had already signed up with Storm – the same modelling agency that had added Kate to its

---

37 'Kate and Lottie Moss to become *Vogue*'s first cover sisters', Charlotte Griffiths, *Daily Mail*, 21 August 2014.

books back in 1988. Lottie had also (again following in the footsteps of her big sister) been photographed for Calvin Klein – shot by Michael Avedon, the grandson of Richard Avedon, who photographed the iconic 1980 Calvin Klein Jeans campaign starring a fifteen-year-old Brooke Shields, with the tagline 'You want to know what comes between me and my Calvins? Nothing.' When *Teen Vogue* asked Lottie during an interview what had inspired her to become a model, she pointed at her illustrious older sister. 'Well, it kind of runs in the family. Kate was a massive part of why I started,' said the younger Moss.[38]

As with so many top jobs in modern Britain, a future at a top modelling agency was a family affair. The younger Moss was one of the 'Sads', or Sons and Daughters – as the maverick journalist Julie Burchill labelled them – the children of privilege who, as if by magic, had snapped up the same cushy jobs as their older relatives. It would be unfair to single out the Moss clan. In recent years, plenty of other Sads have appeared on Britain's collective radar.

---

38 'Kate Moss' little sister made her catwalk debut', Ella Alexander, *Glamour*, 10 March 2015.

There was Rafferty Law, the son of Jude Law and Sadie Frost (modelling contract); Romeo Beckham, the son of David and Victoria (2013 face of designer brand Burberry); Brooklyn Beckham (stint as a photographer for Burberry); Pixie Geldof, daughter of Bob Geldof and Paula Yates (model, singer and socialite); not to mention Pippa Middleton, the younger sister of the Duchess of Cambridge (columnist and author). Flick through any newspaper or glossy magazine in Britain today and the chances are the children of privilege will be staring straight back at you. It may be the precocious relatives of actors, models and musicians – children like Lottie Moss and Romeo Beckham. It might be a columnist for your favourite newspaper. It could even be the politician you voted for at the last election. Either way, public life in Britain is increasingly dominated by the sons and daughters of money.

This trend is not confined to the sorts of jobs that dominate the *Evening Standard* gossip columns. A glance at the state of the professions similarly betrays a country dominated by an affluent elite. Just 7 per cent of Britons are privately educated, yet according to a government report published in 2014, 33 per cent of MPs,

71 per cent of senior judges and 44 per cent of people on the *Sunday Times Rich List* attended fee-paying schools. Almost half (43 per cent) of newspaper columnists and a quarter (26 per cent) of BBC executives were products of the private school system, too. Not that it is strictly the progeny of Britain's highly exclusive private school network who are seamlessly peculating up into the professions. While Oxford and Cambridge graduates comprise just 1 per cent of Britain's population, according to the aforementioned report they make up 75 per cent of senior judges, 59 per cent of Cabinet ministers, 47 per cent of newspaper columnists and 12 per cent of the *Sunday Times Rich List*.[39] A nationally representative survey of 1,026 people conducted by the market research firm GfK for the BBC found further evidence of a closed shop at the top. Using seven social classes,[40] the study found that over twelve times as many

---

39 'Closed shop at the top in deeply elitist Britain, says study', Andrew Sparrow, *The Guardian*, 28 August 2014.

40 The seven categories: elite, established middle class, new affluent workers, technical middle class, traditional working class, emerging service workers, precariat.

of the elite in 2011 came from the most privileged backgrounds compared to those from the precariat. Just
11 per cent of the elite had risen from the lowest social
class.[41] The Sutton Trust, which has been carrying out
surveys of Britain's professions for over a decade, has
talked of the 'staying power of the privately educated
at the top of the UK's professional hierarchy'. In its
2016 annual report, it found that almost three-quarters
(71 per cent) of top military officers were educated privately, while 61 per cent of Britain's top doctors were
educated at independent schools (another 22 per cent
attended grammar schools).[42]

Even the music industry, which once gave expression
to working-class authenticity, is increasingly dominated
by the children of privilege. In 2011, music magazine
The Word revealed that 60 per cent of UK chart acts
were either privately educated or from exclusive stage
schools. This compared unfavourably with 1990, when

---

41 *Social Class in the 21st Century*, Professor Mike Savage, op. cit.

42 'Leading People 2016', Sutton Trust, 24 February 2016, http://www.
suttontrust.com/researcharchive/leading-people-2016.

the magazine found that nearly 80 per cent of artists in the Top 40 went to state schools.[43] Acting appears to be faring even worse, with cut-glass accents and fatuous self-confidence increasingly ubiquitous. Award-winning British actors are more than twice as likely as award-winning pop stars to have been educated privately. Almost half (42 per cent) of British Bafta winners went to independent schools, while the same is true of just 19 per cent of British winners at the Brit Awards. As the actress Julie Walters recently explained, 'I look at almost all the up-and-coming names and they're from the posh schools ... Don't get me wrong ... they're wonderful. It's just a shame those working-class kids aren't coming through.'[44] According to the BBC controller of drama commissioning Ben Stephenson, 'Acting has become a very middle-class profession because it's too expensive to become an actor.'[45] Chairman of the Arts

---

43 'Has pop gone posh?', Tom Bateman, bbc.co.uk, 28 January 2011.

44 'Julie Walters warns of a future where only "posh" can afford to act', Andrew Hough, *Daily Telegraph*, 3 September 2012.

45 'Class a big issue in arts, says BBC drama boss', Hannah Furness, *Daily Telegraph*, 23 August 2014.

Council Peter Bazalgette has similarly complained that the number of actors from public school is now 'out of proportion' with society.

Sport appears to be going the same way. Just a third of top athletes went to state schools, despite the fact that 93 per cent of children in Britain receive their education in the state sector.

The exclusivity of the elite is perhaps most glaring in politics. After leaving Oxford, David Cameron got his first job at the Conservative Research Department because Lord Lexden, who at the time worked there as Deputy Director, received a telephone call from Buckingham Palace tipping him off about 'an outstanding young man'.[46] Behind Cameron stands a Cabinet which is largely made up of millionaires. According to the *Telegraph*, the combined wealth of the Cabinet in 2012 was nearly £70 million, with eighteen out of twenty-nine ministers millionaires.[47] The back benches are similarly

---

46 'Conservative MP: How the Queen secured my selection for the party', Tim Walker, *Daily Telegraph*, 10 March 2012.

47 'Exclusive: Cabinet is worth £70 million', Christopher Hope, *Daily Telegraph*, 27 May 2012.

stuffed with a grossly unrepresentative sample of people. When Margaret Thatcher came to power in 1979, around 40 per cent of Labour MPs had done some form of manual or clerical work before entering Parliament. By 2010, that figure had plummeted to just 9 per cent. The shape of the job market (structural mobility) undoubtedly accounts for some of the change: fewer jobs today are officially classed as 'manual'. Yet the extent to which Parliament has become the talking shop of the middle classes is evident in other ways, too. An astonishing 91 per cent of the 2010 intake of MPs were university graduates, while 32 per cent of the 2015 intake of MPs were privately educated.[48] Parliament is similarly unrepresentative when it comes to gender and ethnicity, though things improved at the 2015 election. According to the 2011 Census, 12.9 per cent of the UK population come from a non-white background, yet non-white MPs make up just 6 per cent of the parliament. Under a third of MPs are female.[49]

---

48 'Leading People 2016', Sutton Trust, op. cit.

49 'Record numbers of female and minority-ethnic MPs in new House of Commons', Helena Bengtsson, Sally Weale and Libby Brooks, *The Guardian*, 8 May 2015.

Yet while there is progress in these areas, in terms of the class composition of the House of Commons, the direction of travel is the other way. As the academic Sean Swan has written for the Democratic Audit website, 'A glance at today's House of Commons will show far more women, openly gay people and BAMEs than in the past, but it will also show more public school boys.'[50]

The decline in social mobility in politics may ultimately have serious consequences. It is increasingly said that the public are 'disenfranchised' with politics because of 'liberal elitism' over issues such as Europe and immigration. There is undoubtedly a degree of truth to this. Outside of London, the ubiquity in politics of what the political scientist Samuel P. Huntington has termed 'Davos man' – rich, cosmopolitan and intensely bourgeois in his tastes – has left many who still value concepts like national identity feeling alienated.[51] But another explanation for the public switching off (literally as well as figuratively)

---

50 'The concept of class is absent from political debate, even as inequality in Britain reaches new heights', Sean Swan, Democratic Audit, 11 February 2016.

51 'Dead Souls: The Denationalization of the American Elite', Samuel P. Huntington, *National Interest*, Spring 2004.

every time a politician opens his or her mouth on television may be found in the increasing domination of politics by a small social class. The increasing allure of populists could boil down in part to their simply looking and sounding a little more like the rest of us.

A lack of social mobility is also evident in the housing market, where inequality is perpetuated by a much-talked-about generational divide. Rarely does a week go past without a report in the media alluding to this 'generation gap'. The increasing penury of the young is said to coincide with the rise of the comfortably off pensioner. According to research by the *Financial Times*, in the 1960s and 1970s, twenty-somethings with average incomes after housing were better off than 60 per cent of the population. Today, the same age group can expect only 37 per cent of the population to have lower incomes than them after housing costs.[52] A major reason for increasing inequality between young and old is the property market. Many older people first got on

---

52 'No country for young men – UK generation gap widens', Chris Giles and Sarah O'Connor, *Financial Times*, 23 February 2015.

the property ladder when it was relatively inexpensive to do so. The average house today costs £283,565 and is forecast to rise to £349,000 by the end of the decade.[53] Meanwhile, the number of property millionaires is set to treble over the next fifteen years[54] (one is created every seven minutes, mainly in London).[55]

The discrepancy in rates of home ownership between young and old has been exacerbated by government policies which have in recent years maintained the so-called 'triple lock' on pensions while cutting benefits for the young and poor. However, it is important not to view this through a strictly generational lens: the class divide is as important as ever. The young have lost out to the old across rich and poor alike, but the losses have been strongest in average or poor families.[56]

---

53 'Number of £1m homes set to triple by 2030 – but first-time buyers will still struggle', Rhiannon Bury, *Daily Telegraph*, 18 February 2016.

54 'House prices: is Aberdeen's slump a portent for London?', *The Week*, 26 February 2016.

55 *Inequality and the 1%*, Danny Dorling, Verso, 1st edition (2014).

56 'Over 50,000 families shipped out of London boroughs in the past three years due to welfare cuts and soaring rents', Daniel Douglas, *The Independent*, 29 April 2015.

Against this backdrop, it is unsurprising that few politicians would be so bold as to claim that Britain is already a meritocracy. To borrow a phrase from George Orwell, Britain is a family with the wrong members in control. Children from working-class backgrounds may occasionally make it to the top in Britain; however, the odds of them doing so are not good. Meritocracy may be the desired destination, but only a foolish or dishonest politician would claim that Britain has the point of arrival in its sights. The real political divide is between those who pay lip service to the radical-sounding mantra of meritocracy and those who really mean it. The former outnumber the latter considerably.

Unless the structure of the economy changes as it did during the post-war period, the absolute rate of social mobility is likely to remain flat for the foreseeable future. A bright but poor child will rarely move up the ladder unless one of his peers higher up passes him on the way down. *There is only so much room at the top.*

Part V

EDUCATION IS THE most important factor in determining whether a child will grow up to be a poor adult. Those with a low level of educational achievement are up to five times more likely to be living in poverty than those who received a good education.[57] It is therefore understandable that politicians should place a great deal of emphasis on better schooling.

That said, education begins long before a child pulls on their first school uniform and passes through the school gates. There is an increasing awareness of this salient truth;

57 'How do childhood circumstances affect poverty and deprivation as an adult?', Office for National Statistics, 23 September 2014, http://www. ons.gov.uk/ons/rel/household-income/intergenerational-transmission-of-poverty-in-the-uk---eu/2014/sty-causes-of-poverty-uk.html.

as a consequence, early years education is better today in Britain than ever before. Ofsted's 'Early Years' report for 2015 found that early education in Britain has 'never been stronger', with 85 per cent of early years settings considered good or outstanding.[58] The report also found significant progress on the part of disadvantaged children.

Yet, despite poorer children's development rising along with that of their more affluent peers, according to Ofsted's report, the attainment gap between rich and poor has not narrowed. On average, poor children have already fallen behind wealthier children by the time they start school. According to the Sutton Trust, children from the poorest fifth of families are almost a year (11.1 months) behind middle-income families in scores on vocabulary tests by the time they are five.[59] Adding to the problem, a government report recently found that fewer than 5,000 schools were providing free early years education to two-year-olds, and those that

---

58 'Early education is better than ever but attainment gap remains', Ofsted, 13 July 2015.

59 'Poorer children a year behind at start of school', Sutton Trust, 1 February 2010.

did were taking a disproportionate number from better-off households.[60]

We will get to schools in a moment. Jumping forward a bit, the chances of going to university – as well as of getting a good degree – depend a great deal on family background. Whether a person goes to university at all – and if they do, which university they attend – has a substantial impact on that person's opportunities and earning potential later in life (not to mention on the advantages won through the friendship networks formed at university). Graduates can earn up to £12,000 a year more than their non-graduate peers – the equivalent of more than £500,000 over an average working life. University confers other, less obvious benefits too. Graduates are less likely to commit crime, drink heavily or smoke and are more likely to educate their own children well. They are also less likely to discriminate against people of different sexualities and from different ethnic backgrounds.[61]

---

60 'Early education is better than ever but attainment gap remains', Ofsted, op. cit.

61 'Higher education: it's good for you (and society)', Jack Grove, *Times Higher Education*, 2 November 2013.

In recent years, higher education has expanded considerably. Meanwhile, the number of young people with no qualifications at all has fallen dramatically. However, the expansion of educational attainment is still spread unequally across the population. The bottom fifth of the population are 40 per cent less likely to go to university than those from the top fifth.[62] Of those who started university between 2004/05 and 2009/10, students from less affluent backgrounds are more likely to drop out and less likely to graduate with a good degree than their peers from more affluent backgrounds. This remains true even for those studying the same subjects and with the same A-level results.[63]

The expansion of university education has also arguably created a two-tier system of higher education, with the employment prospects of students attending the new universities (the former polytechnics) significantly

---

62 'Socio-economic differences in university outcomes in the UK: drop-out, degree completion and degree class', Claire Crawford, Institute for Fiscal Studies, October 2014.

63 'Students from poorer backgrounds do less well at university', Nuffield Foundation, 4 November 2014.

worse than those attending traditional institutions. There are over 150 universities in the UK; however, they were not all created equal. In the past decade, while the number of students from poorer backgrounds going to university has risen, the proportion attending one of the Russell Group universities – an elite group of twenty-four institutions, including Oxford, Cambridge and Imperial College London – has actually fallen.[64] Around one in six (17.2 per cent) students from lower socio-economic groups started a course at a Russell Group university in 2015. This compares with nearly one in three (32.1 per cent) of their wealthier peers. The most advantaged 20 per cent of young people are around seven times more likely[65] to attend these more selective higher education institutions than the most disadvantaged 40 per cent. Graduates of the traditional universities are also far more likely to end up in the elite than those

---

64 'The Proportion of Poorer Students Studying At UK's Top Universities Has Fallen', Lucy Sheriff, Huffington Post UK, 18 February 2016.

65 'State of the nation 2013: social mobility and child poverty in Great Britain', Social Mobility and Child Poverty Commission, October 2013.

who attended former polytechnic institutions.[66] In a striking example of closed-shop Britain, a disproportionately large number of places at Oxford are taken up by people with Norman Conquest surnames such as Baskerville, Darcy, Mandeville and Montgomery.[67] This is not because a Norman surname confers great wisdom; rather, it is because we live in a society where privilege begets privilege. Wealth, power and the opportunity to attend a top university are seemingly handed down the generations like a sacred family heirloom.

Top employers tend overwhelmingly to recruit from this narrow section of the population, focusing almost exclusively on the most prestigious twenty universities out of a possible 115 when searching for new talent. As a consequence, for all the myth-making in Britain about entrepreneurialism and 'self-made' men and women, in terms of elitism, the top echelons of British business resemble the professions – both are stuffed

---

66 *Social Class in the 21st Century*, Professor Mike Savage, op. cit.

67 'You don't need a posh name for Oxford or Cambridge, but it does help', David McKie, *The Guardian*, 30 October 2013.

with people from highly exceptional backgrounds. In 2014, excluding those who were educated abroad, 41 per cent of British-educated FTSE 350 CEOs and over half (60 per cent) of those in the *Sunday Times Rich List* were privately educated. Almost half (43 per cent) of FTSE 350 CEOs attended a top Russell Group university.[68]

The introduction of tuition fees has not, as initially feared, resulted in fewer students from working-class backgrounds applying to go to university. But against such institutional partiality, it is worth questioning the efficacy of a policy that will see many poorer students, who are far less likely to attend the elite institutions, saddled with mountains of debt for what amount to second-rate degrees.

For those unable to afford a gap year, on leaving university the world of work beckons. Journalism provides an illustrative case of how the professions are increasingly colonised by the middle classes in a world where a degree on its own is not enough. It also demonstrates

---

68   'Elitist Britain?', Social Mobility and Child Poverty Commission, 28 August 2014.

how the expansion of higher education has disproportionately benefited the children of the elite. The next
time you hear a plummy-voiced commentator holding
court on a television current affairs programme, understand that it is probably because just 3 per cent of today's
journalists have parents in unskilled occupations. This
compares with 17 per cent of the public as a whole.
In contrast, almost two-thirds (65 per cent) of journalists
have parents who are 'professionals, managers, direc-
tors, or senior officials' – compared with 29 per cent
of the public.[69] Whereas at one time journalism offered
a well-structured career path for bright working-class
kids, a job in the media today is increasingly something
that only a child with affluent parents can aspire to.

A number of factors explain the transformation of
journalism into a largely middle-class pursuit – factors
which might equally apply to other professions. More
and more, the newspapers rely on free labour for their
content, including unpaid interns and impressionable
young people willing to write copy for nothing on the

---

69   'State of the nation 2013', op. cit.

promise of supposedly career-benefiting 'exposure'. This gives an in-built advantage to those from middle-class and wealthy backgrounds who can afford to take unpaid internships and spend time churning out articles for nothing. London is now the unpaid intern capital of Europe, and in journalism it shows. According to a recent survey by the National Council for the Training of Journalists, 83 per cent of journalists who started work in the three years prior to the survey did some sort of work experience or an internship before getting their first job, 92 per cent of which were unpaid. The average length of the unpaid work was seven weeks, with a quarter lasting more than three months.[70] In other words, almost four-fifths of budding journalists gained a career advantage unavailable to working-class kids for whom mere 'exposure' would never pay the bills.

Like many of today's jobs, a career in journalism is also increasingly dependent on academic qualifications. One side effect of this saturation of the undergraduate market has been the new importance attached to

70 'Journalists at Work', NCTJ, February 2013.

expensive postgraduate qualifications. As access to a university education has expanded, so greater value has been placed on education beyond a Bachelor's degree. This throws up yet another hurdle to underprivileged students. A Master's in journalism at the highly desirable City University in London costs around £8,000 – a sum not covered by regular student loans. And this is before living costs are factored in. Attending one of the best universities often means that money must be found to live in London, the city with the most expensive living costs in the country. A small minority of students invariably get lucky and are offered a charitable grant to help pay their way through their studies. Most students, however, will be forced to go cap in hand to the commercial banks. If at some point in the past they have besmirched their credit report, the bank will invariably turn them away empty handed. If they do get lucky and the bank does lend them the money, another large stipend must then be put aside to cover six months of unpaid work at a leading newspaper.

Economic reproduction of the elite, as illustrated by the above example, goes hand in hand with the influence of what the French sociologist Pierre Bourdieu described as 'cultural capital'. If a budding young journalist *does* manage to score an interview after all of the above, there is the small matter of middle-class employers unconsciously favouring middle-class applicants. As the editor of the *Press Gazette* Dominic Ponsford has pointed out, middle-class editors tend to appoint people who are superficially like them.[71] This is not confined to journalism (nor to class similarities). Research in the United States has found that employers seek candidates who are 'not only competent but culturally similar to themselves'.[72]

Cultural capital often goes together with social capital. The networks people form – of colleagues, neighbours, even lovers – can allow the transmission of capital to those in a particular social milieu while excluding those outside of it. Put more straightforwardly, if you live in London and have friends in high-powered jobs, you are far more likely to get an 'in' with someone influential in your

---

71 'Why journalism has become "most exclusive middle-class profession"', Dominic Ponsford, *Press Gazette*, 20 July 2009.

72 'If You Want To Get Hired, Act Like Your Potential Boss', Drake Baer, *Business Insider*, 29 May 2014.

desired profession than someone who lives a long way from the capital and who lacks the same contacts. In 1973, the American sociologist Mark Granovetter published a pioneering piece of research on the influence of what he termed these 'weak ties' (acquaintances as opposed to family members and close friends).[73] In what was to become one of the most cited papers ever written, Granovetter found by conducting numerous interviews that a majority of new jobs were acquired with the aid of 'weak ties'.

In the modern vernacular, the process of hungrily obtaining these weak ties is recognised and encouraged as part of the process of 'networking'. And networking takes on an increased importance the higher up the job market one looks. Anyone can walk into a job centre and locate a job cleaning toilets or driving an HGV lorry. However, many professional jobs – in business, journalism and law – are rarely advertised publicly at all, and rely heavily on relatively insular networks when searching for new recruits. Weak ties are everything.

---

73 'The Strength of Weak Ties', Mark S. Granovetter, *American Journal of Sociology*, vol. 78, issue 6, May 1973.

The strength of weak ties in contemporary Britain was reiterated in an analysis at the LSE of the recent Great British Class Survey. Those who worked in professional occupations were found to be far more likely to know others in similar occupations – and fewer people in working-class jobs. A similar pattern was apparent when researchers looked at the weak ties of manual workers. Analysing the data, the LSE's Professor Savage concluded that, while social classes were less sealed off from one another than fifty years ago, 'Poorer people know far fewer people in high-status jobs than do their better-off neighbours.'[74]

Beyond some dystopian regimentation of British society, it is hard to see how the power of these sorts of social networks could ever be completely diminished. In non-capitalist societies, patronage networks exercise an even greater influence on who fills desirable jobs and who gains access to the material rewards conferred on the elite. The best jobs invariably go to those with the best connections to the ruling party or dictator. Even in

---

74 *Social Class in the 21st Century*, Professor Mike Savage, op. cit.

ostensibly progressive organisations here in Britain, networks often form on the basis of who exhibits the correct political 'line' on various ideological matters. It is hard to see this as an advance on the existing establishment networks of patronage.

There are of course things that governments and individual companies can do to negate the influence of networks. However, there is nothing – beyond solutions most of us would find unpalatable – that either government or private industry can do to completely eradicate them. Which is perhaps why a greater emphasis is usually placed by politicians on the state of Britain's schools.

Part VI

GRAMMAR SCHOOLS ARE one of the most enduring educational myths. For some, they represent the obvious answer to Britain's social mobility conundrum. A great deal of this nostalgia rests on an assumption I have already touched upon – that social mobility was markedly better in Britain during the post-war period and is now in precipitous decline. A number of senior Conservatives support the opening of new grammar schools – as do the UK Independence Party. Some on the left, such as the journalist Nick Cohen, have also advocated a return to grammar school education in order to give a leg up to 'the poor with brains'.[75]

---

75 'Long live grammars', Nick Cohen, *The Guardian*, 31 July 2005.

Proponents of a return to grammars genuinely want to improve the education chances for working-class kids – or at least most of them do.

Part of the attraction of the old system undoubtedly rests on the fact that stark inequalities exist in comprehensive schooling. Despite the formal abolition of selection, in practice it persists, and, as with elsewhere in the economy, the power of money has only increased in recent decades. Homes in desirable school catchment areas cost significantly more than those in areas with unpopular schools. According to a recent survey of 1,100 parents of school-age children, parents are willing to pay 18 per cent more for a property near their preferred school – the equivalent of £32,000 on the average property price of nearly £180,000 in England, Wales and Scotland.[76] In London, the premium is £77,000 on a house costing £474,000. For parents who wish to spend even greater sums educating their children, there are exclusive fee-paying (independent)

---

76 'One in four families move house to secure school place – survey', Richard Adams, *The Guardian*, 2 September 2015.

schools. Approximately 7 per cent of children in education attend these schools, and fees start at around £3,000 per annum.[77] However, this initial investment offers a handsome return. Pupils who attend fee-paying schools are five times more likely to go on to study at Oxford than their peers from the state sector.

Half a century after a Labour government first moved to abolish grammar schools, there is no equality in education. The most deprived areas in Britain have 30 per cent fewer good schools than the least deprived. There are also fewer good teachers who want to work there.[78] According to the OECD, British schools are some of the most socially segregated in the developed world.[79] Such is the demand for school places that ambitious mothers have reportedly started registering their unborn

---

77 'Fee-paying schools: bargain hunting', The Good Schools Guide, https://www.goodschoolsguide.co.uk/help-and-advice/choosing-a-school/fee-paying-schools-bargain-hunting.

78 'State of the nation 2013', op. cit.

79 'UK schools "most socially segregated"', Sean Coughlan, bbc.co.uk, 11 September 2012.

children for prestigious private schools.[80] Other affluent parents 'hot house' their children from the age of three by paying for costly private tutoring. William Petty, the co-director of Bonas MacFarlane, which provides private tutoring, recently told the *Times Educational Supplement* that Britain had 'the most in-demand private [schools] sector in the world'.

The private school network imbues in the children who attend a level of social and cultural capital that has the power to open invisible doors as they grow older. It should come as no surprise to learn that so many parents want to send their children private when they are subsequently likely to earn £193,700 more on average between the ages of twenty-six and forty-two than those who attend state schools.[81]

Accounting for family background and early educational achievement, the wage premium is still a massive £57,653. Children from independent schools who

---

80 'Unborn babies join queue for school places', Javier Espinoza, *Daily Telegraph*, 20 February 2016.

81 Ibid.

didn't go to university are just as likely to enter the elite as working-class Oxford graduates who attended comprehensives.[82]

As discussed already, Michael Young's polemic against meritocracy was originally aimed at the grammar school system, which was seen to epitomise the ruthless separation of 'gifted' pupils from the rest at an early age. *The Rise of the Meritocracy* thus caricatured the 11-plus examination – essentially an IQ test – as operating on the assumption that, in Young's words, 'Civilisation does not depend on the stolid mass ... but upon a creative minority ... The restless elite.' Those who passed the 11-plus were unpityingly separated from the stolid mass and set on a path to future prosperity. It might have been meritocratic in the formal sense, but it was hardly egalitarian – a single test taken aged eleven was used to justify vastly different outcomes throughout adulthood. Calls to bring back grammar schools are often based on similarly inegalitarian assumptions: the sheep must be ruthlessly sorted from the goats in the name of

---

82   *Social Class in the 21st Century*, Professor Mike Savage, op. cit.

'social mobility'. The most commonly heard defence of the grammar school system is that once upon a time it allowed bright working-class kids to transcend their home life. This is the definition of the meritocratic ideal. In passing the 11-plus, the 25 per cent of children who did get to go to grammar schools could leave their less gifted peers behind and percolate up into the professions.

When grammar schools were first introduced, there were in fact good meritocratic reasons to support educational reforms. A large divide between the type of secondary education available to the rich and the poor led in 1944 to the Education Act, which introduced the so-called 'tripartite' system of education. This included grammar schools, secondary modern schools and technical schools. The different schools were intended to provide separate but equal schooling geared to children of different abilities. In practice, few technical schools were actually built; thus, for most children it was a case of passing the 11-plus or attending a substandard secondary modern. The inequalities perpetuated by the tripartite system – most working-class children ended up at secondary moderns – led to the formation of the comprehensive movement, which campaigned on the principle of one type of secondary education for all. This policy was ultimately adopted by the Labour Party, resulting in Harold Wilson's government asking local education authorities in 1965 to reorganise secondary education along comprehensive lines. At the time, it was felt that selective education was on the way out. Doubt was increasingly being cast on theories of inherited intelligence; gender inequality was rife – many local education authorities had more grammar school places for boys than girls; and middle-class dissatisfaction with the system was growing. Thus, when Labour Education Minister Tony Crosland reportedly promised in the 1960s to 'destroy every fucking grammar school in England, Wales and Northern Ireland', there was no eruption of popular outrage.

By 1979, over 80 per cent of secondary school pupils were attending comprehensive schools. In a neat historical irony, it was Margaret Thatcher as Education Secretary who, between 1970 and 1974, is understood to have closed more grammar schools than any Education Secretary before or since. The former Tory leader

Sir John Major went on to make a doomed attempt to rally voters in the 1997 election around the slogan of 'A grammar school in every town!'; however, on the whole, few mainstream politicians have seriously considered reintroducing grammars (perhaps voters realised that Major's policy would also have meant a secondary modern in every town). Between 1980 and 2015, the Conservatives did not open any new grammar schools and nor did Labour close any existing ones. The matter was understood to have been finally closed in 2007 when the young Tory leader David Cameron rejected calls to bring back grammars, defining it as a 'key test' of whether the Conservative Party was fit for office[83] (though in 2015 Cameron appeared to row back on this early pledge, allowing his Education Secretary Nicky Morgan to approve a so-called 'satellite' grammar school in Sevenoaks in Kent – the first grammar school to be approved for fifty years).[84]

---

83 'Cameron steps up grammars attack', bbc.co.uk, 22 May 2007.

84 'New Kent grammar school in Sevenoaks to be approved by Education Secretary Nicky Morgan following Weald of Kent Proposal', Kent Online, 15 October 2015.

Yet the egalitarian penumbra surrounding grammar schools still lingers around British political life like a bad smell. It is undoubtedly bound up with feelings of social mobility and optimism that characterised the post-war period of the twentieth century. It was then that the professions were expanding and the whiff of equality was in the air. A school system that was seen to cater to the different 'types' of pupil was instituted along supposedly scientific lines. If you were clever enough, you could pass the 11-plus and stand a fighting chance against wealthy graduates from the private schools. Names of the famous alumni of the grammar school system are often dropped, in order to contrast the seemingly boundless social mobility of that era with today's gilded elite. Both Harold Wilson and the former Conservative leader Michael Howard attended grammar schools, as did Margaret Thatcher and Sir John Major. In contrast, both Tony Blair and David Cameron were educated at independent schools. Perhaps the most radical thing about the grammar school system from today's perspective is that selection did not rely on parental wealth. The grammar schools did not care where pupils lived.

A child could attend the local grammar school because they had passed a test, not because their parents could afford to pay the premium on a property near the school. A recent piece of research found that basing admissions on closeness to a school was one of today's main drivers of educational inequality in Britain.[85]

Yet much of the romanticism surrounding grammar schools is misplaced. In fact, selection at eleven still exists in thirty-six local authorities; and the evidence gleaned from the 164 remaining state-funded selective schools is a damning indictment of the grammar school system. A recent study of Buckinghamshire, a county with a wholly selective school system, found that private school pupils were two and a half times more likely to pass the 11-plus exam than state school pupils. Conversely, the pass rate for children on free school meals was one-eighth of the average.[86] This discrepancy between wealthy pupils and the rest occurred in spite of

---

85 '"Local schools" drive inequality', Sean Coughlan, bbc.co.uk, 6 October 2014.

86 'Grammar schools do not boost social mobility, report finds', Sarah Cassidy, *The Independent*, 16 October 2015.

the introduction of supposedly 'tutor-proof' testing in 2013. The rich still managed to pay private tutors to beat the 11-plus. Areas that have retained selective education also have a bigger average wage gap between high and low earners. The highest earners from grammar school areas were found to be better off than top earners born in comparable comprehensive authorities.[87]

Grammar schools may benefit the 20 to 25 per cent of pupils who attend, but education for the rest tends to suffer. And these losers come disproportionately from poor homes. Meanwhile, despite the meritocratic mythology, the winners of the grammar system come overwhelmingly from the affluent middle classes. A study by the Sutton Trust found that just 3 per cent of those attending existing grammar schools were entitled to free school meals. Almost 13 per cent of entrants came from the independent sector, largely made up of fee-paying preparatory schools.[88] At 161 out of the UK's 164 grammar

---

87 'Grammar schools create wider pay gap, research finds', Richard Adams, *The Guardian*, 29 May 2014.

88 'Grammar schools – Sutton Trust fact sheet', http://www.suttontrust.com/wp-content/uploads/2015/10/GRAMMAR-SCHOOLS-FACT-SHEET.pdf.

schools, only 10 per cent of pupils were eligible for free school meals. Meanwhile, ninety-eight of these schools had fewer than 3 per cent and twenty-one had fewer than 1 per cent.[89] According to the Institute for Fiscal Studies, deprived children are significantly less likely to get into a grammar school than the most privileged, even when they achieve the same grades aged eleven.[90]

Thus the old myth about grammar schools lifting up bright members of the working class does not stand up to scrutiny. Selection benefits the affluent but results in poorer academic performance for the rest. Educational performance for the poorest pupils in areas where selection persists is *significantly* worse than their equivalents in comprehensive areas. Nor do global comparisons reflect favourably on grammar schools: nine of the ten best education systems in the world are comprehensive.[91]

---

89 '5 reasons why a return to grammar schools is a bad idea', Policy Exchange, 5 December 2014.

90 'Entry to grammar schools in England for disadvantaged children', Jonathan Cribb, Luke Sibieta and Anna Vignoles, Institute for Fiscal Studies, 8 November 2013.

91 'Grammar schools – do they really help social mobility?', Helen Barnard, Joseph Rowntree Foundation, 19 October 2015.

Grammar schools ultimately fail on their own terms. They may benefit the affluent middle classes, but there is no evidence – either from the past or in the present – to suggest that they help the poor. [92] Far from boosting social mobility as their champions claim, grammar schools are a 1950s throwback mired in empty romanticism.

In a different sense, grammar schools resemble the doctrine of meritocracy in microcosm. Even if grammars were able to achieve what their supporters claim – a high degree of social mobility for the poor – the ethical question engendered by their success would remain: does a just society anoint a handful of people based on the extremely narrow criteria of IQ?

When looked at this way, it is perhaps less surprising that so many proponents of a return to grammar schools are on the political right: the desire to return to educational selection is part of a conservative desire to justify economic inequalities on the basis of natural ability. Unjust rewards are considered just if they occur as a result of merit. The fly in the ointment, so to speak, is a familiar one:

---

92 'Grammar school myths', Chris Cook, *Financial Times*, 28 January 2013.

a scientific IQ test may seem egalitarian, but to para-phrase Marx, children sit the critical 11-plus examination 'under circumstances given and transmitted from the past'. The weight of vastly divergent home and educational experiences is invariably brought to bear on rich and poor children, producing contrasting human material at the age of eleven. The intention may be to sort the sheep from the goats, but a good number of goats are able to use the advantage accrued by their parentage to pass as sheep. Not all sheep are treated equally, either. When grammar schools reached their zenith in the late 1950s, fewer than 0.3 per cent of pupils leaving grammar school with two A-levels had come from the unskilled working class. Richard Tawney pointed out this fundamental paradox, which is at the heart of the 'equality of opportunity' rhetoric, way back in the 1930s.[93] 'It is only the presence of a high degree of practical equality which can diffuse and generalise opportunities to rise,' Tawney wrote. 'The existence of such opportunities ... depends not only on an open road, but upon an equal start.'

---

93 *Equality*, R. H. Tawney, op. cit.

The same paradox that has upset broader attempts to engender social mobility also applies to grammar schools and the 11-plus. In 1961, Raymond Williams effectively summed up the problem of a selective school system thus:

> Differences in learning ability obviously exist, but there is great danger in making these into separate and absolute categories. It is right that a child should be taught in a way appropriate to his learning ability, but because this itself depends on his whole development, including not only questions of personal character growth but also questions of his real social environment and the stimulation received from it, too early a division into intellectual grades in part creates the situation which it is offering to meet.[94]

Unequal outcomes generate unequal opportunities. Educational selection at age eleven is ultimately liable to become a self-fulfilling prophecy.

---

94   *The Long Revolution*, Raymond Williams, Chatto & Windus, 1st edition (1961).

Part VII.

Part VII

INCOME INEQUALITY HAS increased rapidly in Britain since the late 1970s. The unstoppable advance of the so-called 1 per cent has been compounded in the public mind by austerity. Why, after all, should ordinary people suffer when a small minority appear to be doing so well? Originating in a 2006 documentary about the growing gap between a wealthy American elite and the rest of society, the term '1 per cent' has spawned an extensive literature on both sides of the Atlantic. Its corollary – 'We are the 99 per cent' – was the slogan adopted by the influential anti-capitalist protest movement Occupy Wall St.

Political grumbling about inequality never went away, of course, but the global financial crash of 2008 dragged it firmly back into the mainstream. A cataclysm largely caused by the reckless lending of American banks was – and in fact still is – being paid for by austerity programmes that disproportionately hit the poorest. It was not *their* crisis, yet, in Britain at least, the poor have been asked to pick up the tab for it. While those struggling saw cuts to social security under the 2010–15 coalition government, the top rate of income tax was lowered from 50p to 45p. Similarly, in 2014, the average FTSE 100 chief executive in Britain earned 140–150 times the wage of the average worker. In the United States, around 95 per cent of 2009–12 income gains went to the wealthiest 1 per cent.[95]

This is not a situation in which, as some politicians maintain, there is no money left. In fact, there is quite a lot of money sloshing around, but it is overwhelmingly being hoovered up by a small percentage of people at the top.

When inequality is discussed, there comes a point in the conversation when the debate invariably turns

---

95 'Some 95% of 2009–2012 Income Gains Went to Wealthiest 1%', Brenda Cronin, *Wall Street Journal*, 10 September 2013.

to the supposedly innate personal qualities of the rich. The elite are where they are, so it is argued, because they possess both the ability and the drive to succeed. If a disproportionate number of the rich are the products of an elite upbringing, well, that is because talent is distributed throughout society unevenly and is often hereditary. The former Mayor of London Boris Johnson articulated something along these lines when in 2013 he told the Centre for Policy Studies that inequality was the product of human beings who are 'far from equal in raw ability'[96] (though he also said that more should be done to help talented people from working-class backgrounds 'rise to the top').

So are the elite simply cut from a different cloth to the rest of us?

Intelligence is certainly to some extent inherited. Experiments with identical and fraternal twins (the former share the same DNA and the latter don't) consistently show that the IQs of identical twins are far

---

96 'Boris Johnson: some people are too stupid to get on in life', Peter Dominiczak and James Kirkup, *Daily Telegraph*, 27 November 2013.

more similar in their scores than fraternal twins.[97] As Stuart Richie, the author of *Intelligence: All That Matters*, puts it, 'The only possible reason for this is genetic: after all, the only thing that differs between the two types of twins that would make them more similar – so long as each pair is raised in the same family – is the percentage of genes they share.'[98] Ritchie goes on to say that, on average, around 50 per cent of the reason people vary on intelligence scores is genetic.

At the controversial end of debates like this is the 1994 American book *The Bell Curve* by the political scientists Richard Herrnstein and Charles Murray. The central thesis of the book is that intelligence is responsible for the trajectory of a person's life, and that a deficient IQ is typically the best explanation for poverty. The book proved controversial when it came out, not only because of its reiteration of discredited eugenicist arguments from the nineteenth century – that the 'cognitive elite'

---

97 *Intelligence: All That Matters*, Stuart Richie, Hodder & Stoughton, 1st edition (2015).

98 Ibid.

was being out-bred by a multitude of halfwits – but also because it argued that different ethnic groups possessed varying levels of intelligence. For those who took the work of Herrnstein and Murray seriously, a society like the United States was immensely unequal because it was a genetic meritocracy. Blacks were poor not because of historic racism and class oppression, but because they were stupid. While the whiff of racism discredited those sections of the book that dwelt on the supposed innate difference in intelligence of different ethnic groups, in conservative circles *The Bell Curve* remains influential. And, from the political perspective of the largely white elite, one can see why: a thesis that purports to justify economic and racial privileges as neatly as *The Bell Curve* contains some obvious attractions for those who are doing well out of existing inequalities.

Of course, few would argue that human beings are born equal in every respect. Most of us, however much we might practise at kicking a football around a field, will never obtain a fraction of the skill possessed by a player like Argentina's Lionel Messi. Similarly, it is possible to acknowledge the presence of intellectual genius without crudely disparaging it as a mere upshot of a wealthy upbringing.

Yet, a closer look at the disadvantages accrued by poorer children early on in their lives explains why there is more to success than intelligence alone. Environmental mechanisms exist that can turn a dull child into an average one and an average child into a successful one. The inverse is also true. Heritability interacts with a person's surrounding environment, and there is evidence to suggest that underprivileged environments can hamper a child's intellectual potential regardless of that child's innate IQ. Poverty steals time and saps focus. It can also create a disorderly environment. A child who spends a great deal of the day hungry or worrying about money will already be at a disadvantage when compared to his or her more affluent peers. Heritability also tends to be higher in children from wealthier families.[99] In an influential 2003 article, Eric Turkheimer, a sociology professor at the University of Virginia, noted that many of the twins

---

99   Ibid.

who had hitherto been used in studies of IQ had come from middle-class families.[100] As a result, Turkheimer went in search of data applicable to twins from a broader range of families. Looking at an appropriate mixed study of 50,000 American children, the professor found that among the poorest families, the IQs of identical twins contained just as much variety as the IQs of fraternal twins. Put another way, poverty had an appreciable influence on what were previously thought to be innate characteristics. As Turkheimer would later tell the *New York Times*, 'If you have a chaotic environment, kids' genetic potential doesn't have a chance to be expressed. Well-off families can provide the mental stimulation needed for genes to build the brain circuitry for intelligence.'[101]

When it comes to inequality, only a lunatic would argue for *total* economic equality. The central objection to this is a familiar one: how can complete equality exist

---

100 'After the Bell Curve', David L. Kirp, *New York Times Magazine*, 23 July 2006.

101 Ibid.

without force? And if there must be an enforcer, how does that person remain equal to everyone else?

One can accept this yet still recognise that vast inequalities can have a substantial impact on which cornflakes make their way to the top of the packet, however vigorously that packet is shaken.

There is another, often-overlooked point. Michael Young's dystopia is unbearable because large inequalities are justified on the basis of a set of supposedly infallible criteria. Whereas economic supremacy was hitherto attributed to good fortune, in the meritocracy such fortuities have been eliminated. The new society still rises on the crooked backs of the poor; yet it has meticulously sorted the deserving from the undeserving using the unimpeachable IQ test. As in the past, the underclass still sinks like a stone; however, the entrepreneur has been freed from his bondage of having to bequeath to the poor man any of his miserly charity. The rich man is still in his castle and the poor man remains, as ever, loitering forlornly at his gate. But now the meritocracy has made them high and lowly, and ordered their estate.

Part VIII

A N UNGENEROUS INTERPRETATION of left-wing history might argue that an ungrateful British working class, seduced by Thatcherism and New Labour, failed to live up to socialist expectations and so the left moved on like a bored lover to those deemed more deserving of its support. To paraphrase the much-paraphrased Bertolt Brecht, in recent times the working class has shown little interest in overthrowing capitalism and has thus been dissolved in favour of a new proletariat. Class analysis, at one time the *raison d'être* of the socialist movement, has been usurped on the left by the grievances of women, gays and ethnic minorities. The personal is supposedly political, and as a consequence being a radical today relates as much to who you are as to what you think.

In reality, identity politics was an understandable response to the injustices of the twentieth century and the defeats suffered by the left. Despite the loftiness of much left-wing rhetoric, sexism, racism and homophobia have never successfully been eliminated from socialist politics because these movements have invariably reflected the societies in which they were conceived. It has often been made apparent to women in particular that the priorities for leftists lay strictly within the class framework. The brotherhood has traditionally taken precedence over the sisterhood, and marginalised groups have been urged to wait until the chains of capitalism have been thrown off before issuing their demands. The struggles against misogyny and other forms of discrimination have rarely been undertaken with the same vigour unleashed against capitalist bosses.

It would be wrong to imply that today this dynamic has been turned on its head. One can still find sexism, racism and homophobia on the left as easily as one can find it in wider society. In an article for *Slate* about the US Democratic primaries, Michelle Goldberg wrote in late 2015 about a cultural phenomenon of so-called Bernie Bros – male supporters of US presidential candidate Bernie Sanders who 'seem to believe that their class politics exempt them from taking sexism seriously'.[102] The sexual assault allegations that embroiled the British Socialist Workers' Party in 2013 paints an even grimmer picture of self-proclaimed egalitarians who see no contradiction in using their power as men to belittle and abuse women. In this wretched incident, despite serious allegations of sexual assault being made against a senior party member of the SWP – 'Comrade Delta' – the female accusers were discouraged from going to the police on the basis that socialists should have 'no faith in the bourgeois court system to deliver justice'.[103]

Again, rudimentary women's rights had to wait until the victory of the glorious revolution.

---

102 'Men Explain Hillary to Me', Michelle Goldberg, *Slate*, 6 November 2015.

103 'Ranks of Socialist Workers Party are split over handling of rape allegation', Jerome Taylor, *The Independent*, 11 January 2013.

Nor is 21st-century Britain a meritocratic utopia for women and ethnic and sexual minorities. A gender pay gap evidently exists,[104] even if there is a debate to be had over its size. Young black men are incarcerated in Britain at a much higher rate than young white men and are far more likely to be living in poverty.[105] It is fashionable to emit a liberal sneer at the flagrant racism of the American justice system, but according to the Equality and Human Rights Commission, there is now greater disproportionality in the number of black people in prisons in the UK than in the US.[106] Despite the state's recognition of gay marriage, there also remain areas of Britain – and particularly within minority communities – where being openly gay is to risk physical injury or even death.

That said, discernible progress is being made in terms of liberal equality. Inequalities based around identity

---

104 Equal Pay Portal, http://www.equalpayportal.co.uk/statistics.

105 'Inequality, housing and employment statistics', Institute of Race Relations, http://www.irr.org.uk/research/statistics/poverty.

106 'Prison: the fact', Prison Reform Trust, summer 2013 briefing, http://www. prisonreformtrust.org.uk/Portals/0/Documents/Prisonthefacts.pdf.

are narrowing; indeed, they have never been narrower. But economic inequality is growing and with it so is class inequality. Paradoxically, it is the latter which is increasingly ignored.

Identity politics has, as the African-American academic Adolph L. Reed[107] has written, tended to exaggerate the partial nature of the victories achieved through greater inclusiveness – not to mention through the policing of language. The progress made towards eliminating various forms of discrimination is welcome in its own right. However, on its own it is a change the economically privileged can live with. Put another way, identity politics is compatible with neo-liberal economics. It can co-exist with the corporate boss who makes more money in a week than his cleaner takes home in a year – as long as the chances of being the boss are assigned proportionally among different ethnic groups, sexualities and genders. Individual winners and losers remain as remote from each other as ever; they are simply sorted

---

107 '"To unite the many": an interview with Adolph L. Reed, Jr', Gregor Baszak and Spencer A. Leonard, The Platypus Affiliated Society, April 2015.

in direct proportion to their numbers in society. As with the idea of meritocracy, the ultimate aim of identity politics is to 'tune up' the elite rather than to abolish it.

By emphasising difference over commonality, identity politics also makes it harder for the left to establish a mass politics based around shared economic interests. By seeking constantly to divide people up into smaller and smaller groups, identity politics forestalls the creation of a sense of unity around issues of economic justice. And because it is obsessed with difference, the divisions are potentially endless. In this way it functions like a mild strand of nationalism. The tribe always comes before the class, even if below the surface the interests of the tribe are wildly disparate.

All of this matters to this discussion because identity politics is fostering a creeping disregard for the impact social class can have on a person's life chances. An assumption that white males invariably occupy an economically privileged position seems to be the ubiquitous view among those pushing for greater diversity in the professions. Most equality drives today explicitly exclude class. A random Google search of the words 'media diversity' immediately throws up several examples. 'Is the media industry sufficiently diverse?' asks a headline on the BBC website from December 2014.[108] And this is a perfectly reasonable question. Yet the proceeding 700-word article makes not a single mention of opening up the media to people from working-class backgrounds. A similar piece, published a few weeks earlier in the *New Statesman*, nicely captures the liberal conceit surrounding equality. In an article entitled 'The British media has a terrible problem with "surface diversity"', the author advances her own form of 'surface diversity', contrasting 'ethnic minorities who simply can't afford [a journalism internship]' with 'affluent, middle-class white candidates' who apparently can.[109] For the writer of the piece, it was taken as read that white students were 'affluent' whereas ethnic minority students were not.

The diversity agenda can be similarly partial in the US.

---

108 'Is the media industry sufficiently diverse?', bbc.co.uk, 30 December 2014.

109 'The British media has a terrible problem with "surface diversity"', Monisha Rajesh, *New Statesman*, 14 October 2014.

According to the influential Leadership Conference on Civil and Human Rights, 'A diverse media is one that is inclusive of minorities and women in content.'[110] This is unarguably true. Yet, if the media is to be truly diverse, it ought also to be a profession that is inclusive of economically disadvantaged men, even if they do happen to be white.

White males are certainly over-represented in many of the most prestigious professions in both Britain and the United States. However, this is an over-representation of a very particular class of white male. White men from the working class are not – by a long stretch – ubiquitous in the elite. In fact, they encounter economic hurdles *at least as difficult* to surmount as the barriers of gender and racial equality faced by their contemporaries. A six-month unpaid internship at a prestigious newspaper – or an unpaid internship in any job, for that matter – is as off limits to a white working-class boy as it is to anyone else who lacks the sufficient funds. Professor

---

110 'Media Diversity: Frequently Asked Questions', The Leadership Conference, http://www.civilrights.org/action_center/media-diversity/faq.html.

Savage's analysis of the British Class Survey found evidence of a social class pay gap comparable to the gender pay gap that rightly induces so much opprobrium in liberals. Those from the most elite backgrounds were often paid as much as 25 per cent more than those from more modest backgrounds for doing the same work.[111] Equality of opportunity along the lines envisioned by proponents of identity politics would be an unquestionable improvement on the status quo. Equality gains of any sort are not to be sniffed at. Too often, women and minorities have been shut out from or discouraged from entering certain professions, and putting this right is self-evidently a positive thing. There is also a burgeoning tendency among conservative commentators to lionise the 'white working class' based on the fact that the latter supposedly reject the values of a 'metropolitan liberal elite'. Such arguments are often made by commentators who have never shown the same level of concern for supposed working-class values when those values have threatened (at least in the abstract) their own

---

111 *Social Class in the 21st Century*, Professor Mike Savage, op. cit.

economic power. The white working class are thus of rhetorical value – but only as long as they remain caricatures who sit at home swilling lager and sticking two fingers up at 'political correctness'. As soon as they go on strike or attend a protest they are rendered invisible (or invariably denounced as 'Luddites'). This attempt to square off the white working class against others in society is not so much a negation of identity politics as an attempt to play the game on behalf of a competing interest group.

As we have seen, the working class has taken a noticeable backseat in left-wing discourse in recent years, usurped by the various 'liberation' struggles. This has occurred at a time when (if the thesis of stalling social mobility is correct) class is *at least as* significant a factor as both gender and ethnicity in understanding disadvantage.[112] There is even a danger that, in excluding any recognition of class from the processes enacted to tackle entrenched racial and gender privilege, working-class people who fail to tick the correct boxes could be

---

112 'State of the nation 2013', op. cit.

left even further behind. We can see this in its linguistic form among young activists for whom denouncing 'white men' is considered radical. Indeed, railing against the supposed pampered existence of this demographic has become the stock-in-trade of many activists. But it isn't only among activists that penniless white men are viewed pejoratively. According to a recent study of British attitudes, British people typically expect white men to be drunk, lazy, rude and promiscuous.[113] Never mind that a significant proportion of the precariat in Britain – the new economic underclass with the odds stacked firmly against them – are themselves white.

This is testament to how far class has fallen out of debates around inequality – and it is starting to make itself felt in falling voter turnout. Half of C2 voters and 59 per cent of D–E voters backed Labour at the 1997 general election. By 2015, this figure had dropped to 32 per cent of C2 voters and 41 per cent of D–E voters. While turnout at general elections is falling more

---

113 'Lazy, drunken, promiscuous, rude … why the UK loves to hate young white men', Mike Savage, *The Guardian*, 19 December 2015.

generally, turnout among working-class voters is falling at a faster rate.[114]

The increasing invisibility of class in debates around inequality – and the symptomatic lumping together of 'white men' – is happening at a time when white children from poorer backgrounds, especially boys, are falling behind every other ethnic group at school. According to a recent review of progress towards greater equality in Britain by the Equality and Human Rights Commission, despite life becoming fairer for many in recent years, for other young people and, in particular for white working-class boys, 'life on many fronts has got worse'.[115]

One doesn't need to single out boys in order to understand how the benefits of liberal identity politics are not being distributed equally. For many years, a lot more men than women went to university. Things have thankfully changed since then. By the late 1980s, young

---

114 'How Britain voted in 2015', Ipsos MORI, 26 August 2015.

115 'Largest ever review reveals "winners and losers" in progress towards equality in Great Britain', Equality and Human Rights Commission, 30 October 2015, http://www.equalityhumanrights.com/largest-ever-review-reveals-%E2%80%98winners-and-losers%E2%80%99-progress-towards-equality-great-britain.

men and women went to university in roughly equal numbers. During the 1980s, the proportion of middle-class women going to university nearly tripled, from 6 per cent to 15 per cent. A triumph, you might think, for the liberal interpretation of diversity. Yet during the same period, the proportion of women from the lowest 20 per cent of the income scale going to university failed to increase at all – it actually remained flat at 6 per cent.[116] For the class-blind proponents of liberal identity politics, gender equality in the university admissions process had been achieved. Yet, despite this ostensible victory, the odds of going to university remained as firmly stacked as ever against working-class women – not only on the basis of their gender, but on the basis of the class they were born into.

As well as ignoring the disadvantages accrued by a background in the working class, liberal identity politics throws up other problems. One of these is the common assumption that ethnic and gender groups form a homogeneous bloc. This is reflected in commonly

---

116 'David Willetts speech on grammar schools', *Daily Telegraph*, 16 May 2007.

espoused commentary about a supposed 'black community' or 'gay community', or in the implied notion that female voters should automatically pick female politicians at the ballot box. Essentialism of this sort erroneously ascribes homogeneity to what in reality are divergent groups with different interests. As should be fairly obvious, beyond the extremes, entire populations are not reducible to a single viewpoint. When it comes to self-appointed spokespeople for these 'communities', the assumption that membership of a particular group confers a special insight in terms of the interests of that group is a recipe for demagoguery.

Progress in terms of liberal equality is discernible, if only in the coverage equality issues are starting to receive in the mainstream. Even the Conservative *Daily Telegraph* talks today of David Cameron's 'women problem'. As of March 2016, all new contracts in the current Conservative government's Department for Transport will include gender equality targets.[117] Meanwhile, getting

---

117 'Government demands gender equality in transport sector', Gwyn Topham, *The Guardian*, 29 January 2016.

more women and ethnic minorities into Britain's board-rooms is considered a centre-ground issue that only those on the lunatic political fringes would dare to oppose. Yet attempts to level the playing field in a similar fashion for the working class brings on a touch of the vapours. When, at the 2014 Labour Party conference, the shadow Equalities Minister Gloria De Piero suggested that public sector employers should monitor the social background of their workers in order to try to end the dominance of the middle classes in the top jobs, the *Daily Mail* commentator Dominic Sandbrook lamented the move as 'not merely absurd, but dangerous'. 'It is essentially a form of social engineering,' Sandbrook wrote, 'which would judge young men and women not by educational achievement, their hard work and potential, but by their parents' background.'[118]

Social democratic politics ultimately proceeds, as Adolph L. Reed has written, from a 'concrete, material base for solidarity – not gestures, guilt tripping and

---

[118] 'Labour's plan to force employers to be biased against middle-class recruits isn't just lunacy, it's immoral', Dominic Sandbrook, *Daily Mail*, 23 September 2014.

idealist abstractions'. The struggle for a fairer, more equal society must ultimately unite disparate groups – white and non-white; male and female; gay and straight – on the basis of a shared lack of economic opportunity. An unemployed black twenty-something living in Peckham does not share the same class interests as a British-Indian property magnate from Manchester. Of course, both individuals are united in their opposition to racism; however, in the political space this is rapidly becoming a moot point when the contemporary Conservative Party is socially liberal and led by a self-described 'liberal Conservative'.[119]

Identity politics is in the ascendant because it fits nicely into society's direction of travel. The saying goes that the left won the cultural war while the right won the economic war. It would be more accurate to say that both left and right have embraced meritocracy. Each side's victories are those which are most compatible with the meritocratic order. There is no meritocratic justification

---

119 'I'm not a deeply ideological person. I'm a practical one', Andrew Rawnsley, *The Guardian*, 18 December 2005.

for keeping ethnic minorities and women out of the boardroom; but similarly, nor can justification be found for taxing the bonuses of the elite once superficial 'equality' has been achieved.

Class politics must certainly evolve with the times – at the very least it should take account of the legitimate grievances of people who feel marginalised for reasons other than their class. It must also recognise that today's class distinctions are not always the categorical divisions of the past. However, liberal identity politics is increasingly a zero-sum game – a game in which 'white men' must invariably lose out so that women, ethnic minorities and LGBT individuals can prosper. With no account for the impact of class, this will simply give rise to another injustice; or, more accurately, it will compound an existing one. As in Michael Young's meritocratic dystopia, Britain's individual winners and losers will continue to occupy vastly different worlds and will remain firmly pitted against each other in the sharp-elbowed race to the top.

Part 3

Part IX

BRITAIN IS A considerable distance from being able to call itself a meritocracy. Fears of meritocratic dystopia are thus comparable to worrying about how to spend a lottery fortune while stood in the queue waiting to purchase a ticket. Such trepidation can at least wait until the public schools are trembling under the weight of working-class entrants and the top professions are a little less dominated by the upper crust.

Britain has some of the worst levels of social mobility in the developed world. Genuine equality of opportunity would require a genuine radicalism – radicalism of a kind that British politicians are unwilling to countenance. A proper commitment to free and fair competition among people would require, as a start, a dilution in the power of inherited wealth and the hobbling of the private schools as well as the hereditary influence more generally – things the vast majority of politicians are unlikely to support. In 2013, one in five children in Britain lived in a home that was cold or damp. One in twenty households could not afford to feed their children properly.[120] Last year, almost two-fifths of teachers said they had seen children who had not had enough to eat turning up for lessons.[121] Another recent poll found that nearly half of teachers had taken food in to school to feed ravenous pupils.[122]

Against this backdrop, all talk of meritocracy brings to mind Richard Tawney's characterisation of those who preach equality of opportunity while '[resisting] most strenuously attempts to apply it'.[123] Here is located

---

120 *Breadline Britain: The Rise of Mass Poverty*, Steward Lansley and Joanna Mack, Oneworld, 1st edition (2015).

121 'More pupils turning up to school "hungry and unable to concentrate"', *Daily Telegraph*, 9 January 2015.

122 'Pupil hunger: nearly half of teachers have taken food in for their pupils', Emma Drury, *The Guardian*, 19 June 2012.

123 *Equality*, R. H. Tawney, op. cit.

the fissure on the left between those who genuinely seek to create a socially mobile society and those who pay lip service to it while pursuing policies antithetical to a meritocratic order. Because New Labour's verbal commitment to social mobility lacked a corresponding drive to reduce inequality, its rhetoric gave off a strong whiff of cognitive dissonance. Thus, after thirteen years of Labour governments, Britain remained a society dominated by the privileged and, invariably, the children of the privileged. If social mobility was not notably worse in 2010 than it was in 1997, it was not demonstrably better either. The acceptance by New Labour of large inequalities of wealth, buttressed by the radical-sounding mantra of equality of opportunity, produced a society in which the odds remained firmly stacked against those from poorer homes. The sociologist Pierre Bourdieu caricatured the sort of meritocratic formula favoured by liberal politicians as resembling a game of roulette. Rather than social life functioning as an accumulation of history, in the eyes of the meritocratic elite, life resembles a game of chance in which every moment is independent of the previous one.

This imaginary sphere of equality of opportunity is 'a world without inertia, without accumulation, without heredity or acquired properties … [where] every soldier has a marshal's baton in his knapsack, and every prize can be attained, instantaneously, by everyone, so that at each moment anyone can become anything'.[124]

In this reading of events, the 'baggage of history' has been casually flung into Trotsky's famous dustbin of history as if it were an old sock. Only the meritocrats are seemingly incapable of recognising that human beings are – at least to some extent – products of their own histories.

Arguments around social mobility should therefore be reconnected to the problem of economic inequality. Reams of evidence suggest that social mobility is fundamentally incompatible with the sorts of economic inequalities that persist across Britain. The privileges of the parents tend overwhelmingly to become the privileges of the children. Opportunities denied to the poor disproportionately fall into the laps of the well-off.

---

124 'The forms of capital', Pierre Bourdieu, 1986, https://www.marxists.org/reference/subject/philosophy/works/fr/bourdieu-forms-capital.htm.

A significant degree of social mobility between the working and middle classes exists, but at the very top, the equivalent of an invisible admissions process locks out those from disadvantaged backgrounds. Trying to fashion a meritocracy from a society as grossly unequal as our own is a bit like applying a coat of paint to a crumbling old house. It may project a wholesome veneer; it may even induce in the owner feelings of smug satisfaction; ultimately, however, the old cracks fester under the surface and are noticeable to anyone who sets foot inside. Inequality produces unequal prospects. Social mobility promotes inequality and reinforces unequal prospects. Social mobility therefore negates itself. *Inequality + social mobility = inequality of opportunity*. As a stand-alone objective, meritocracy is an unattainable fantasy. A meritocracy would be a deeply unpleasant place to live for large numbers of people. It would also cannibalise itself through the unequal outcomes it generated. Politicians are thus chasing a mirage.

The dystopian aristocracy of talent envisioned in *The Rise of the Meritocracy* would simply create a new set of discontents. At times, there is a greater degree of honesty among commentators on the right about what a genuine meritocracy might look like. Back in 1960, it was free-market guru Friedrich Hayek who recognised that 'a society in which it was generally assumed that a high income was proof of merit and a low income of the lack of it ... would probably be much more unbearable [to unsuccessful people] than the one in which it was frankly recognised that there was no necessary connection'.[125] In a true meritocracy, those at the bottom would face the double indignity of knowing beyond all doubt that they fully deserved their fate. Extreme inequality would be considered fair and would thus produce 'a more wounding, stratified system perhaps than had been known since the days of slavery', as Young put it. Meanwhile, at the top of the ladder, wealthy individuals would see no reason to eschew their privilege. After all, if society has been comprehensively reordered on a rational basis so that the new elite has qualified for its dominion, why lose sleep over the condition of the poor?

---

125 *The Constitution of Liberty: The Definitive Edition (Collected Works)*, Friedrich A. Hayek, University of Chicago Press (2011).

This is of course a moot point. Equal opportunity will always be illusory because differentiation is a natural part of growing up. No government could equalise the quality of a child's parenting even if it wanted to. Equality of opportunity is thus a utopian fantasy.

Michael Young's work offers us another reason to fear a sleek and well-oiled meritocracy. Britain today resembles Young's dystopia only in the sense that disproportionate rewards are showered on the elite and contempt is increasingly shown to those at the bottom.

Young predicted that meritocratic arguments would ultimately be used to justify large economic inequalities. By attributing poverty to personal failure, meritocracy is invariably useful in attempting to justify excessive rewards. Meritocracy may not exist in the Britain of 2016, but increasing numbers of people share the assumptions of the meritocrats. A 2013 YouGov poll found that 85 per cent of respondents thought teenagers fifty years ago needed better-placed parents to get on in life than they do today.[126] Despite this country having

---

126 'Britain's middle-class meritocracy', Peter Kellner, YouGov, 24 June 2013.

comparatively poor levels of social mobility when measured against other developed nations, Britain is one of the few countries in Europe in which a majority of people believe that the actions of the individual – rather than forces beyond their personal control – determine success.[127] You might say that Britain is becoming more like the United States in terms of how we view success.

This is reflected in a growing belief that the poor lack resources due to personal failings. In recent years there has been a hardening of attitudes toward the recipients of welfare. According to a recent British Social Attitudes Survey, poverty today is increasingly seen as the fault of the individual, rather than as a reflection of larger processes. Support for spending on welfare has declined significantly in the past three decades.[128]

The more meritocratic Britain becomes (or, to be more precise, the more Britain believes it is a meritocracy),

---

127 'Ever higher society, ever harder to ascend', *The Economist*, 29 December 2004.

128 'Public attitudes to poverty and welfare, 1983–2011', Elizabeth Clery, Lucy Lee and Sarah Kunz, Joseph Rowntree Foundation, https://www.natcen.ac.uk/media/137637/poverty-and-welfare.pdf.

the less sympathy there will likely be for those who find themselves at the bottom. If you believe that poverty is mainly caused by personal imprudence, you are less likely to want to see the government spend money trying to alleviate it. Similarly, if you expect to possess riches in the near future – or, more accurately, if you believe that the opportunity to do so is equally open to all – you are less inclined to want to impose higher taxes on the rich. This version of the meritocratic ideal is embodied in its purest form in the so-called American dream – the notion that success is open to every American citizen, regardless of ethnic or socio-economic background. The American author John Steinbeck once observed that socialism never took off in the United States because the poor saw themselves not as an exploited proletariat but as temporarily embarrassed millionaires. Voting to tax the rich would be to risk making a rod for your own back. American culture is littered with anecdotal examples of the 'self-made' individual who has successfully managed to pull himself up 'by the boot straps'. The self-help industry is worth $10 billion a year in the US and thrives on the repackaging of trite slogans such as James Allen's 'Circumstances do not make a man; they reveal him.'[129] Ultimately, however, the industry functions like a sprinkling of sugar spread over a foul-tasting dessert: along with Britain, America is one of the least socially mobile countries in the developed world.

Rather than pining for this illusory ideal, British politicians would do well to turn the vision of a ruthless meritocracy on its head. Social mobility should be the by-product of a society that treats everyone well, rather than an end in itself. The evidence is clear: greater economic equality would allow for the development of every individual along truly meritocratic lines. More equal societies tend to have better rates of social mobility.[130]

We can of course concede that people are born of different stock. But we might also allow individuals to thrive in their own unique ways. If ability is largely

---

129 'The Self-Help Industry Helps Itself to Billions of Dollars', Lindsay Myers, Brain Blogger, 23 May 2014, http://brainblogger.com/2014/05/23/the-self-help-industry-helps-itself-to-billions-of-dollars.

130 'Intergenerational Mobility in Europe and North America', Jo Blanden, Paul Gregg and Stephen Machin, Centre for Economic Performance, April 2005.

hereditary, as some maintain – if there really is a 'cognitive elite' – should those who inherit low ability be condemned to a bleak and wretched life based on what is, in essence, the mere lottery of genetics? The knowledge that a good portion of human intelligence is innate ought instead to create *more* – not less – of an imperative to look after those who lack the requisite raw material to join the higher-ups. Machines are not yet the new race of slaves, and therefore a degree of drudgery is inherent in any contemporary economy. A more egalitarian society would ensure that everyone could live well, whereas a meritocratic society would endlessly remind the drudges of their worthlessness. A just society is thus not a meritocratic one.

There ought to be no shame in not wanting to compete or in being found to lack the requisite 'merit' to do so. Cast out the meritocracy and there needn't be disgrace in knowing your station.

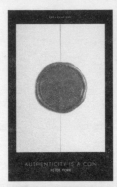